ANTHOLOGY

— for —

MUSIC IN THE RENAISSANCE

Western Music in Context: A Norton History

Walter Frisch SERIES EDITOR

Music in the Medieval West, by Margot Fassler

Music in the Renaissance, by Richard Freedman

Music in the Baroque, by Wendy Heller

Music in the Eighteenth Century, by John Rice

Music in the Nineteenth Century, by Walter Frisch

Music in the Twentieth and Twenty-First Centuries, by Joseph Auner

ANTHOLOGY
— for —
MUSIC IN THE RENAISSANCE

Richard Freedman

Haverford College

W. W. NORTON AND COMPANY

NEW YORK · LONDON

W. W. Norton & Company has been independent since its founding in 1923, when William Warder Norton and Mary D. Herter Norton first published lectures delivered at the People's Institute, the adult education division of New York City's Cooper Union. The firm soon expanded its program beyond the Institute, publishing books by celebrated academics from America and abroad. By midcentury, the two major pillars of Norton's publishing program—trade books and college texts—were firmly established. In the 1950s, the Norton family transferred control of the company to its employees, and today—with a staff of four hundred and a comparable number of trade, college, and professional titles published each year—W. W. Norton & Company stands as the largest and oldest publishing house owned wholly by its employees.

Editor: Maribeth Payne
Associate Editor: Justin Hoffman
Assistant Editor: Ariella Foss
Developmental Editor: Harry Haskell
Manuscript Editor: Bonnie Blackburn
Project Editor: Jack Borrebach
Electronic Media Editor: Steve Hoge
Marketing Manager, Music: Amy Parkin
Production Manager: Ashley Horna
Photo Editor: Stephanie Romeo
Permissions Manager: Megan Jackson
Text Design: Jillian Burr
Composition: CM Preparé
Manufacturing: Quad/Graphics-Fairfield, PA

W. W. Norton & Company, Inc., 500 Fifth Avenue, New York, NY 10110-0017
wwnorton.com
W. W. Norton & Company, Ltd., Castle House, 75/76 Wells Street, London W1T3QT

1 2 3 4 5 6 7 8 9 0

CONTENTS

CONCORDANCE
— for —
MUSIC IN THE RENAISSANCE

PREFACE

This anthology of musical works is a companion to my book *Music in the Renaissance*, which is part of the series Western Music in Context: A Norton History. The anthology includes scores and analytical commentary for excerpts from a broad range of compositions and can be used on its own or in conjunction with *Music in the Renaissance*. I have chosen selections for their beauty, for the artistic and intellectual developments they engage, and for the availability of a variety of excellent recorded performances.

In *Music in the Renaissance*, like other books in the series, analytical and stylistic discussion of music is expressly kept to a minimum. Yet, no true appreciation of music can be gained by studying social or intellectual context alone; we must engage with the actual notes. The commentaries in this anthology explore the scope and stylistic diversity of music during the fifteenth and sixteenth centuries. They are not intended to be exhaustive, but rather invite instructors and students to explore further the works at hand.

Selections appear in the order of their discussion in *Music in the Renaissance* and support the historical narrative of that text. Several of the pieces presented here are significant to more than one historical development (*Mille regrets*, for instance, is part of the chapter devoted to Josquin des Prez, but it also is considered in the chapters "Number, Medicine, and Magic" and "Music and the Literary Imagination"). See the Concordance for a list of ways to use the anthology in conjunction with the individual chapters. But the pieces also tell their own stories, as explained in their accompanying commentaries, which relate details of source traditions, aspects of structure and representation, and finally the challenges of performance and interpretation.

Most of the scores presented here come from standard scholarly editions. A few have been newly transcribed directly from original sources. As modern editions, they differ from the original sources in various ways: assembling parts into modern score, reducing original note values, adding *musica ficta*, and making choices about text placement. The scores are in many ways indispensable for modern readers. But it is important to return to the original sources, particularly in the case of works from the fifteenth century. Excerpts from some of these original sources can be seen in the book itself. Many other sources are freely available in digital facsimile on the Internet thanks to projects undertaken by the great research libraries of Europe and the Americas; my website (linked from books.wwnorton.com/books/Music-in-the-Renaissance) lists many of these facsimilies. Chapter 2 of *Music in the Renaissance* offers an explanation of the basic concepts of rhythmic notation, the tone system, and musica ficta as they were understood by Renaissance musicians, all useful in studying facsimiles.

A wide range of recording options gives students and instructors flexibility in listening to anthology selections. StudySpace, Norton's online resource for students, provides links to stream nearly every anthology selection from the Naxos Music Library (accessible via an institutional or individual subscription), as well as links to purchase and download recordings from iTunes and Amazon. Many of the anthology selections (especially the most famous ones) have been recorded numerous times; comparing different recorded interpretations can be a revealing exercise in its own right.

Translations are my own unless otherwise noted. Throughout I have aimed to give readers a good sense of the original text in ways that will be useful in the analysis or interpretation of the musical settings.

I am grateful to Leofranc Holford-Strevens for permission to use his revised translation of the text of Du Fay's motet *Supremum est mortalibus*, and to Bonnie Blackburn for many other suggested improvements to the translations. My thanks to Adam Crandell, Music Librarian at Haverford College and to Donna Fournier, Music Librarian at Swarthmore College, for making non-circulating materials available to me in preparing this collection.

ANTHOLOGY

— *for* —

MUSIC IN THE RENAISSANCE

LUCA MARENZIO (1553/54-1599)

Liquide perle
Madrigal, 1580

Edited by Richard Freedman. Modern edition prepared from Luca Marenzio, *Il Primo libro de madrigali a cinque voci* (Venice: Angelo Gardano, 1580), p. 1.

Liquide perle Amor da gl'occhi sparse	*Liquid pearls Love brought from my eyes*
In premio del mio ardore,	*As reward for my desire;*
Ma lass'ohimè, che 'l core	*But alas, my heart*
Di maggior foco m'arse.	*Burned me with greater fire.*
Ahi! che bastava solo	*Ah, if only the first searing pain*
A darmi morte il primo ardente duolo.	*Had been enough to cause my death.*

Published in Luca Marenzio's *First Book of Madrigals for Five Voices* (1580), *Liquide perle* is among the most famous of the composer's many secular works. It was frequently reprinted, arranged, and adapted. The Roman priest Giovenale Ancina even transformed it into a religious *contrafactum*, with a new text, as *Fiamme di vero amore* (Flames of True Love).

At the heart of the poem by Lelio Pasqualino is the paradoxical tension between the "liquid pearls" and the "greater flame" they cannot quench; in combination, the two do not consume each other but are instead resolved only in the speaker's metaphorical "death." We also see this kind of literary tension in other serious madrigals (settings of secular poetry in Italian, and later English), notably Jacques Arcadelt's *Il bianco e dolce cigno* (Anthology 17). Here, as there, the text is cast in rhymed lines of seven and 11 syllables, a versification scheme long favored by Italian poets of the sixteenth century (the overall scheme could be diagrammed as **ABBACC**).

The setting unfolds according to three large poetic ideas, each contained within its own couplet, that seem to have captured Marenzio's musical interest. Each of these large units is marked by some strong articulation. The break between lines 2 and 3, just before "Ma lass'ohimè," coincides with a strong cadence to A. The musical texture shifts from the animated rhythms of measures 14–15 ("burning") to the slow-moving, staggered entries of measures 17–19 ("But alas"). Likewise, the syntactic break at the end of line 4 (m. 30) aligns with a similar textural change from homorhythmic writing to slow-moving counterpoint. This change is also undercut by the subtle way in which Marenzio forges a cadential connection between the two sections: the listener hears the new texture in measure 31 as the completion (in the tenore and basso parts) of a cadence to C that was strongly implied in the previous measures, but never directly realized (see the cadential suspension formula between the top two voices in mm. 29–30). It is an audacious move by the standards of sixteenth-century practice, but one that aptly captures the speaker's exclamatory outburst as he rushes into the last lines of the poem.

Keeping this large-scale design in mind, we can now return to some of the nuances of Marenzio's approach to the images and ideas in the poem. On one hand, the "liquid pearls" are amplified in a series of entries that seem to paint the text as an image in sound. The lively imitative texture of the opening gives way to homorhythmic writing for the top two and the lowest parts at measure 14—a brief passage in the style of the popular canzonetta, which itself melts into a solid cadence to A on the last syllable of "ardore" (at the end of line 2 of the poem). Here Marenzio suddenly turns the musical tables. "But alas," the speaker stumbles, and as he does Marenzio puts an end to lively rhythm.

Now the texture is full, densely contrapuntal, and filled with affective half steps and leaps that force us to share the burning sensation of a heart ablaze. The tonal palette has changed, too, for already with the introduction of the G♯, F♯, and C♯ needed to form the cadence to A, Marenzio has left behind the musical space of the opening couplet, with C, F, and G now replaced by C♯, F♯, and G♯. Later still (in mm. 37–38), Marenzio returns to explore the other extreme, touching not only on F but also briefly on B♭.

Marenzio's contemporaries were aware of the contrasting expressive dimensions of the flat, or "soft," tones (such as B♭ and F) and the sharp, or "hard," tones (like G♯, F♯, and C♯). (See the discussion of "soft" and "hard" tonal positions in the context of hexachords in Chapter 2 of *Music in the Renaissance*.) Gioseffo Zarlino famously advocated these hard and soft tones as fertile material for the musical representation of contrasting affect: hardness was associated with bitterness, softness with effeminacy and sadness. Thomas Morley (see Anthology 3) borrowed Zarlino's advice almost verbatim in his *Plaine and Easie Introduction to Practicall Musicke* (1597). Marenzio's music no doubt appealed to Morley's English readers for its virtuosic ability to put these general ideas into effective practice. Indeed, we can hear some of the same techniques at work in John Wilbye's *Draw on, sweet Night* (Anthology 12).

Marenzio's treatment of the last couplet is especially interesting for the ways in which it combines two lines, each with its own musical idea, in a contrapuntal web of contrasting gestures. On one hand, he joins line 5 ("Ahi, che bastava solo") with a figure that begins abruptly with a held note, then turns in ornamental descent and a tentative half-step cadence (see the canto part, mm. 38–39 and 42–43). Played and replayed against itself, it produces all sorts of interesting suspensions and oblique movement as some parts rise against held notes in others. Simultaneously, he crafts a slow, rising line for the first part of the final line ("a darmi morte"), which is contrapuntally combined with the falling gesture of the previous line (mm. 38–41). The effect nicely underscores the syntactic connection between the words ("ah . . . / had been enough to cause my death"). The melodic figure for "a darmi morte" may also be a reference to the rising melodic profile heard at the outset of the madrigal, musically as well as verbally recalling the "first searing pain" of love.

All of this variety places great demands on the singers. In Marenzio's day, works like these were meant for highly practiced performers—each singing one to a part, and each from a musical text that contained only a single voice part. Marenzio's madrigals (and this one in particular) nevertheless enjoyed very wide circulation among skilled amateurs prepared to meet the challenges of the music.

Doctorum principem

Motet, 1397–1407

O.L. 241

From Johannes Ciconia, *The Works of Johannes Ciconia*, ed. Margaret Bent and Anne Hallmark, Polyphonic Music of the Fourteenth Century, 24 (Monaco: Editions de l'Oiseau-Lyre, 1985), pp. 89–93. The Latin text has been corrected, emended, and translated by Leofranc Holford-Strevens, based on a review of the original manuscript. It thus differs slightly from the Latin text given in the modern edition reproduced here.

CANTUS I

1. O doctorum principem super ethera
reboant virtutum digna merita.
Ergo vive voci detur opera,
promat mentis fervor intus concita.

1. *The fitting merits of his deed extol the prince*
of teachers to beyond the skies. Therefore let
sincerely summoned care be given to living voice,
let fervor of mind show forth.

2. O Francisce Zabarelle, gloria,
decor, honos et lumen Patavorum,
vive felix de tanta victoria;
per te virescit fama proavorum.

2. *O Francesco Zabarella, glory, teacher,*
honor, light of Padua, live contented at such
a triumph. Padua's fame will increase
because of thee.

3. O Francisce Zabarelle, pabula
parasti pastoribus armentorum,
quibus pascant oves: grata secula
te pro munere reboant laborum.

3. *O Francesco Zabarella, thou hast*
provided nourishment for the shepherds
of the flocks, on which they may graze
their sheep. A grateful world proclaims
thee as reward for thy labors.

CANTUS II

1. Melodia suavissima cantemus,
tangant voces melliflue sidera,
concordie carmen lira sonemus,
resonet per choros pulsa cithara.

1. *Let us sing with sweetest melody, let our*
mellifluous voices reach the stars, let us
sound the harmonious lyre, let the plucked
cithara resound throughout the choirs.

2. O Francisce Zabarelle, protector,
imo vetus pater rei publice,
illos ad se vocat rerum conditor
qui fortune miserentur lubrice.

2. *O Francesco Zabarella, protector, yea,*
true father of the commonweal, the
Maker calls unto himself those that
have pity for fleeting misfortune.

3. O Francisce Zabarelle, causas
specularis omnium creatorum;
tuas posteri resonebunt musas
per omnia secular seculorum.

3. *O Francesco Zabarella, thou dost watch*
over the affairs of all creatures: posterity
will resound thy praises for ever and ever.

TENOR

Vir mitis

This complex polytextual motet, with its flowery Latin verses, was written in honor of Francesco Zabarella, archpriest of the cathedral of Padua, where the northern composer Johannes Ciconia worked for a time between 1401 and 1412. Zabarella later became a cardinal, in which capacity he attempted to reconcile the rival factions that supported different popes during the Great Schism in the Catholic Church (1378–1417).

Italian princes and prelates were apparently fond of works like these, with their multiple texts and polyphonic parts. Ciconia composed several others for various patrons and ceremonial events during his long career in Italy. Many of Guillaume Du Fay's occasional motets were likewise written to mark important events in the lives of Italian patrons; see, for instance, his *Supremum est mortalibus* (Anthology 9).

It is not certain whether Ciconia himself had a hand in composing the Latin poetry for *Doctorum principem*. But to judge from the close agreement between the poetic and musical forms, poet and musician anticipated the possibility of such structural correspondence. The two Latin poems follow the same basic scheme: four lines of rhymed couplets, each of which begins with an exclamation. The second and third stanzas of each poem, moreover, open with the same invocation: "O Francesco Zabarella."

Like the text, the motet is divided into three large sections, each corresponding to one of the stanzas of the twin poems. A single slow-moving tenor melody ("vir mitis," a fragment of a plainsong celebrating the gentle qualities of man) serves as the foundation of each section. Its metrical transformations allow it to preserve the same pitch structure but in new temporal proportions. As in many pieces organized around a repeating tenor, the scribe notated this voice part only once, but he provided prose directions (a canon, or "rule") explaining how to sing it in each of three different metrical systems. This kind of order-making was a standard procedure for composers of the years around 1400, who were advised to select a tenor melody, organize it in some way, add appropriate musical counterpoint, and finally work in the poetic texts around the music.

Each of the three large sections opens with wordless flourishes in the upper parts, while the tenor rocks back and forth in open fifths. The three fanfares also "rhyme" with each other musically, beginning and ending with the same vertical sonorities: compare measure 1 with measures 45 and 89, and measure 6 with measures 50 and 94. (The complex time signature in our score starting at measure 89 is an attempt to find modern equivalents for the subtle metrical hierarchies that are fundamental to the original mensural notation. From this point each measure in the modern score consists of either two or three measures of $\frac{2}{4}$ time, and the measure numbers are counted in units of two beats.) These little preludes in turn set up the main business of each stanza. In the first two stanzas the upper pair of voices echo each other, followed by a pause that recalls the end of the wordless introduction (the tenor falls from C to G, while the upper parts form an open sixth above it, just as we heard in mm. 6 and 50). This echoing device is especially effective in the second stanza, where each of the poems opens with Zabarella's name. The third stanza, too, invokes Zabarella's name, but here Ciconia has the two upper parts declaim it simultaneously, just in case we did not get the hint (mm. 96–99).

Throughout the motet a wide range of contrapuntal writing is heard. There are imitative passages, where different words are set to the same music (mm. 8–12, 66–70, and 110–13). There are also brief moments of interlocking texture in which each upper part takes a short rest while the other sings a few notes, or even one note (mm. 43–44). This was an old contrapuntal technique that music theorists of the thirteenth and fourteenth centuries called hocket ("hiccup"). Compared with works of the middle years of the fifteenth century, Ciconia's piece sounds old-fashioned. It has a rather conservative musical texture, with two busy vocal parts over a slow-moving tenor. And when Ciconia forms phrases, his counterpoint strongly favors open fifths and octaves at the beginnings and endings of lines.

Fifteenth-century music books often left many decisions up to performers. No doubt they had the good musical sense to pick a tempo and timbre that suited the space and forces at hand. But such information is not given in the original manuscripts. Nor do these sources offer much guidance on the precise alignment of words and music. Performers were also expected to apply their knowledge of counterpoint in deciding where to sing the unwritten accidentals known as *musica ficta* (false music). Modern editors apply their own understanding of these traditions, adding accidentals above the staff in the case of *musica ficta* (as in the accompanying score) and making educated guesses about which words belong with which notes. The contratenor part does not appear in all sources of the work, and is thus marked as optional by the editors of our score. It nevertheless enriches the sound and texture of the work considerably, as we can hear in the recording by the singers of the early music ensemble Diabolus in Musica. Neither the tenor nor the contratenor carries text, and so they realize the parts with a neutral vocalization. (The musicians of the Ensemble Project Ars Nova also include the contratenor part in their recording, but realize it with a wind instrument rather than vocally.)

THOMAS MORLEY (1557/58-1602)

Miraculous love's wounding
Canzonette, 1595

Edited by Richard Freedman. Modern edition prepared from Thomas Morley, *First Booke of Canzonets to Two Voyces* (London: Thomas Este, 1595), fols. 5ᵛ–6ʳ.

-ing, Are turn'd to ros - es, vi - o - lets and li - lies, vi - o - lets and

-ing, Are turn'd to ros - es, vi - o - lets and li - lies,

li - lies, with o - dour sweet a - bound-ing, sweet a - bound - ing,

vi - o - lets and li - lies, with o - dour sweet a - bound ing, with o - dour

with o - dour sweet a - bound - ing. Mi - ra - cu - lous love's

sweet a - bound - ing. Mi - ra - cu - lous love's wound - ing, love's

wound - ing, mi - ra - cu - lous love's wound - ing mi - ra - cu - lous love's wound -

wound-ing, mi - ra - cu - lous love's wound - ing, mi - ra - cu - lous love's wound -

- ing, mi - ra - cu - lous love's wound - ing love's wound-ing, mi - ra - cu - lous

- ing, mi - ra - cu - lous love's wound - ing, mi - ra - cu-

love's wound - ing, mi - ra - cu - lous love's wound - ing.

lous love's wound - ing, mi - ra - cu - lous love's wound - ing.

Miraculous love's wounding.
E'en those darts my sweet Phillis
So fiercely shot against my heart rebounding
Are turn'd to roses, violets and lilies,
With odour sweet abounding.

A work of deceptive simplicity, *Miraculous love's wounding* was first published in Thomas Morley's *First Booke of Canzonets to Two Voyces* in 1595. (The book was dedicated to his wife's employer, Dame Elizabeth Periam, to whom William Byrd directed his famous set of keyboard compositions, *My Lady Nevell's Booke.*) Like a number of other English madrigals of the day, it was modeled on an Italian source—in this case, a four-voice canzonetta, *Miracolo d'amore* (Miracle of Love), published by the Roman composer Felice Anerio in 1586. Both the text and the music have much in common with Luca Marenzio's *Liquide perle* (see Anthology 1).

English composers like Morley often looked to the Italian peninsula for compositional ideals and literary conceits. Nicholas Yonge's *Musica transalpina* (Music from Beyond the Alps) of 1588 supplied English lyrics for an anthology of the most famous Italian madrigals of the period. Other composers took their turn in arranging, borrowing, or adapting Italian models. For instance, the famous collection that Morley prepared in 1601 for Queen Elizabeth I, *The Triumphes of Oriana*, seems to have been modeled on *Il trionfo di Dori* (The Triumph of Dori), published in Venice in 1592 in honor of a Venetian bride.

Morley's *A Plaine and Easie Introduction to Practicall Musicke* (1597) suggested the duet as an ideal medium for instruction, practice, and private entertainment. It certainly would not be hard to imagine using *Miraculous love's wounding* in such ways. The musical demands are modest: the melodic writing is smooth and generally devoid of awkward leaps; the counterpoint is interesting without being overly dissonant or difficult, and there is little chromaticism. There are no difficult problems of *musica ficta*. Indeed, Morley and his publisher have included accidentals (like the several F♯s) in the notation to show the singers exactly what they need to do to make the cadences to G come out correctly. Throughout the fifteenth century and well into the sixteenth, singers were left to fend for themselves in these situations. Frequent repetition between the voice parts (and economical motivic repetition within them) also made the piece relatively easy to master. Moreover, the equal ranges of the voice parts mean that singing partners could exchange roles, as they do within the piece itself (compare m. 11 with the opening).

Morley's music nicely mirrors the form and ideas of the text. Each of the five lines of poetry is set off with a clear cadence (variously to G, D, and B♭). They are formulaic gestures, to be sure, with rhythmic syncopation and mild, suspended dissonance leading to a resolution at the unison, octave, or third. The moments of greatest tension and release thus serve to reinforce the rhyme scheme. In doing so, they simultaneously give voice to central themes of the poem: the "wounding," the echoes and leaps at "rebounding," and the sheer excess of echoing ornamentation at "abounding." Meanwhile, we are left to wonder about the relationship between the opening line and the remainder of the poem: in bringing it back as a musical refrain, Morley seems to be obsessively replaying the delightful wounds of love.

Par le regart

Chanson, 1450–60

From Guillaume Dufay, *Opera Omnia*, ed. Heinrich Besseler, 9 vols., Corpus Mensurabilis Musicae, 1 (Rome: American Institute of Musicology, 1947–66), 6:88–89. Poetic text quoted from Leeman L. Perkins and Howard Garey, *The Mellon Chansonnier*, 2 vols. (New Haven: Yale University Press, 1979), 2:402.

Par le regard de voz beaulx yeulx	*By the look of your beautiful eyes*
Et de vo maintieng bel et gent	*And [the sight] of your fair and noble manner*
A vous, [belle], viens humblement	*To you, beauty, I come humbly*
Moy presenter, vostre amoureux.	*To present myself, your lover.*
De vostre amour sui desireux	*Of your love I am desirous*
Et mon voloir tout s'i consent	*And all my will consents to it*
Par le regard de voz beaulx yeulx	*By the look of your beautiful eyes*
Et de vo maintieng bel et gent	*And [the sight] of your fair and noble manner*
Or vous plaise, ceur gratieux	*Therefore may it please you, gracious heart*
Moy retenir ore ad present	*To accept me at once*
Pour vostre ami entierement	*As your friend, wholly,*
Et je seray vostre en tous lieux.	*And I will be so everywhere.*
Par le regard de voz beaulx yeulx	*By the look of your beautiful eyes*
Et de vo maintieng bel et gent	*And [the sight] of your fair and noble manner*
A vous, [belle], viens humblement	*To you, beauty, I come humbly*
Moy presenter, vostre amoureux.	*To present myself, your lover.*

Du Fay's song appears in a dozen sources from the second half of the fifteenth century, including the beautiful Mellon Chansonnier, made in Naples by a Burgundian scribe about 1472–75 for Princess Beatrice of Aragon. The poem is a rondeau, one of the old *formes fixes* (fixed forms) fashionable since the 1300s. (See Anthology 5 for an example of a virelai.) Every rondeau shares the same basic formal design, but differs according to the number of lines and rhyme pattern. The overall scheme could be diagramed as **ABaAabAB**, with capital letters indicating the refrain. (**A** rhymes with **a**, and **B** with **b**.) In this poem the refrain is four lines long: two for **A** (lines 1–2), two more for **B** (lines 3–4). It is thus a rondeau quatrain.

Composers of the fourteenth and fifteenth centuries normally crafted their settings of these poems in two sections that correspond to the two halves of the poem. The midpoint was marked by a cadence that allowed singers to repeat the **A** section or continue on to **B** as needed to observe the overall plan of the poem. (The spot is marked with a "sign of congruence" in the two upper voice parts of the Mellon Chansonnier; see Fig. 3.3 in *Music in the Renaissance.*) The uppermost (cantus) voice part carries the musical weight of the song, unfolding as a series of supple melodic phrases, one for each line of text. The tenor part forms a euphonious duet with the cantus, often moving in syncopated parallel sixths until they meet in stable octaves to mark each rhyme. These musical pauses thus serve to emphasize the sonic resemblance of the end-rhymes "beaulx yeulx," "desireux," and "gratieux."

The cadences in this chanson are nevertheless relatively old-fashioned by the measure of many of Du Fay's other songs, particularly in the way the contratenor joins this duet, more or less shadowing the cantus at a fourth below as it approaches a fifth above the final tenor.

It's worth comparing this counterpoint with the very different behavior of the contratenor in Busnoys's *Ja que li ne s'i attende* (Anthology 5); see, for instance, measure 19 of that work, where the contratenor leaps down a fifth as it sounds the lowest tone of the cadence. The new and flexible role for the contratenor exemplified in Busnoys's piece carried important implica tions for polyphonic composition in the fifteenth century, acting as it does much more like a "harmonic" bass line in contexts like this.

It is also interesting to note how the cadences in Du Fay's chanson work in relation to the form and syntax of the poem. The cadence to D in measure 11 marks the midpoint of the poem, where the singers must turn back to repeat the **A** section, as they normally do several times during the rondeau. Heard in the context of the solid cadence to G for the first phrase (m. 6) and its echo at the very end of the piece (m. 23), the pause on D seems to provide a moment of temporary repose.

Elsewhere Du Fay's music exemplifies syntactic patterns that we might otherwise over-look. In measure 15, for instance, he pointedly avoids a cadence at the end of the third line of the refrain ("humblement"), which makes good sense once we realize that the last two lines of the refrain are in fact a single thought. Du Fay's music also undercuts somewhat the final-ity of the last line of the poem by supporting it with an unusual "Phrygian" cadence (mm. 18–19), in which the characteristic approach to the octave has a downward-moving half step in the tenor (B♭ to A), while the cantus moves up by whole step (G to A). This is exactly the opposite of the normal contrapuntal cadence, in which the half step is always in the ascend-ing part. The effect is tentative, even poignant. The coda, with its echoes of the more secure cadence heard in measure 6, brings us at last to a close, even as the speaker obsessively re-turns to the "beautiful eyes" of his beloved. Original fifteenth-century sources often give what seem to be conflicting key signatures in different voice parts (as we find here in Du Fay's chanson). These do not represent a kind of polytonality, despite the impression to mod-ern readers. They instead reflect the different ranges and transposed modes of the different voice parts. It is too vast a topic to take up here, but in fact there is no great conflict among the lines in practice.

Musicians of the fifteenth century understood that each musical phrase (particularly in the cantus part) corresponded to a single poetic line. Given the many ambiguities that swirl around the alignment of text and tone, however, exactly how to distribute the syllables among the notes is a matter of judgment and taste. Modern performers might well come up with a variety of solutions. There has also been much discussion about the role of instruments in this repertory, a subject on which the original manuscripts are completely silent. Earlier scholars argued that the contratenor part, with its wide leaps and quick changes of direction, might have been designed for lute or harp, while the cantus and tenor seemed more vocal in conception. Because the cantus is the most thoroughly texted, some modern groups perform the contratenor, and sometimes the tenor too, on instruments. This approach is taken by the ensemble Diabolus in Musica, which gives the tenor and contratenor parts to a pair of bowed *vielle*s (a kind of fiddle or violin). Nevertheless, other groups perform all three parts of chan-sons like this with voices alone, as we will see in the case of Busnoys's *Ja que li ne s'i attende*.

5

ANTOINE BUSNOYS (1430–1492)

Ja que li ne s'i attende

Chanson, Before 1460

From Leeman L. Perkins and Howard Garey, *The Mellon Chansonnier*, 2 vols. (New Haven: Yale University Press, 1979), 1:71–74; the poetic text is taken from 2:241.

Ja que li ne s'i attende,	*Although he does not hope for it [or, Let Jacqueline wait]*
Car tous aultres sont cassés,	*For all others have been broken,*
Et je l'aime plus qu'assés	*Yet I love him more than enough*
Affin que chescun l'entende.	*For everyone to hear it.*
Ainsi a-il le renon	*Thus he has the reputation*
De porter sur une manche	*Of wearing on one sleeve*
[Deulx des] lettres de mon nom:	*Two of the letters of my name,*
L'une persse et l'aultre blanche.	*One blue and the other white.*
Plus que jamais de sa bande	*More than ever by his side*
Me tiendray, et de si pres	*I will stand, and so closely*
Qu'on verra bien par expres	*That all will see it plainly*
Que tousjours son fait amande.	*That always I'll enhance his state.*
Ja que li ne s'i attende,	*Although he does not hope for it [or, Let Jacqueline wait]*
Car tous aultres sont cassés	*For all others have been broken,*
Et je l'aime plus qu'assés	*Yet I love him more than enough*
Affin que chescun l'entende.	*For everyone to hear it.*

Preserved in a small group of manuscripts compiled in the Loire Valley of France from the 1450s through the 1470s, Antoine Busnoys's chanson points toward the rarefied world of the French-speaking courts of the mid-fifteenth century. The poem is a virelai, another of the traditional refrain forms that fifteenth-century poets took over from previous generations. (See Anthology 4 for an example of a rondeau.) There are two main sections of music: one for the refrain and verse (lines 1–4 and lines 9–12) and another for the two short couplets at the center of the poem (lines 5–8). The overall plan can be diagrammed as **AbbaA**. Musicians of Busnoys's day normally responded to this scheme with two contrasting musical sections—a stable one for the **A** sections, and something more tentative for the **b** sections heard in the middle of the work, sometimes with contrasts in texture or alternative endings, as one can clearly see in the case of Busnoys's chanson.

This setting is richly nuanced on a number of fronts. The hidden meaning of the opening poetic line—run together, the first few syllables can be heard as "Let Jacqueline wait"— is brought out by the music: the four syllables of the otherwise unknown Jacqueline's name are linked in a single melodic phrase in the cantus part, while the contratenor is unusually static. Busnoys also does a nice job of making the listener wait: in each of the first two lines of the refrain, the expected cadence (at mm. 5 and 9) is undercut by the delay or sudden absence of the tenor voice.

In the **b** section of the piece, Busnoys uses musical gestures to underscore the syntactic connection between the pair of couplets, which are really a single thought: "Thus he has the reputation / Of wearing on one sleeve / Two of the letters of my name, / One blue and the other white." In the first ending, the cantus and tenor form a cadence to G, while in the second they come to rest on C. The contratenor plays an especially devious role here: undercutting the first cadence by moving up from D to E (m. 26; sixteenth-century theorists called this an "evaded cadence"), but solidifying it in the case of the second one by leaping from G down to C (m. 30). Indeed, over the course of the fifteenth century the contratenor part in particular was a site of experimentation with new ranges and textural possibilities.

The two endings of the **b** section thus point out the parallelism of the rhyme. They also subordinate the first couplet to the second. The closing figure of the **b** section (m. 30) echoes the cadence heard at the end of the **A** section (m. 19). Last, we should note the incidental touches of imitative counterpoint between the cantus and tenor in the **b** section (mm. 23–30). This idea, too, would come to have a new role as a structural device in later generations.

Busnoys's chanson poses many of the same challenges for performers that we noted in the case of Du Fay's *Par le regart* (Anthology 4). Singers needed to sort out for themselves which syllables belonged with which notes. They also had to decide when to invoke unwritten accidentals. As we noted in the case of the Du Fay chanson, modern scholars and ensembles continue to debate the relative merits and authenticity of using instruments in the performance of chansons of the fifteenth century. The cantus part was clearly intended for vocal performance. But in books like the Mellon Chansonnier it is rare for either the tenor or contratenor part to carry much text, reinforcing the impression of these parts as instrumental rather than vocal on account of their many leaps and pauses. Nevertheless, groups like the Orlando Consort (an all-male ensemble of soloists) perform all three parts vocally, sometimes using neutral vocalizations when the contratenor or tenor cannot support all the syllables of a phrase. The result is extremely musical, and very beautiful.

6

JACOB OBRECHT (1457/58–1505)

Missa de Sancto Donatiano: Kyrie

Cantus-firmus mass, 1487

From Jacob Obrecht, New Obrecht Edition, ed. Chris Maas et al., 18 vols. (Utrecht: Vereniging voor Nederlandse Muziekgeschiedenis, 1983–99), 3:1–5.

MASS TEXT

Kyrie eleison.	*Lord have mercy.*
Christe eleison.	*Christ have mercy.*
Kyrie eleison.	*Lord have mercy.*

LATIN CANTUS FIRMUS TEXT

O beate pater Donatiane pium dominum	*O blessed father Donatian, pray to the loving Lord*
Iesum pro impietatibus nostris deposce.	*Jesus for forgiveness from our sins.*

DUTCH SONG TEXT

Gefft den armen gefangen umb got, dat	*Give to the poor prisoners for God's sake that*
u got helpe mari ut aller not.	*God may help you out of all your need.*

Jacob Obrecht's *Missa de Sancto Donatiano* (Mass for St. Donatian) was commissioned in 1487 as part of a set of memorial services for a pious and wealthy businessman from the Flemish town of Bruges, where the composer was a leading musical figure of his generation. When Obrecht left Bruges for the ducal court of Ferrara in late 1487, he may have taken a copy of the mass with him: the earliest known manuscript was prepared around that time for the Papal Chapel in Rome. The work joins a long line of tenor masses, in which the standard five movements of the Ordinary (Kyrie, Gloria, Credo, Sanctus, and Agnus Dei) are both unified and particularized through a persistent cantus-firmus melody, normally presented in slow-moving notes in the tenor part. (See Anthology 10 and 11 for other examples of tenor masses.)

Obrecht's mass uses not one but two cantus firmi. The first is *O beate pater Donatiane* (O Blessed Father Donatian), a prayer that asks St. Donatian to plead with Jesus on behalf of those who petition him. The tune was probably well known to congregants in late-fifteenth-century Bruges. It certainly meant something to Adriane de Vos, the widow who commissioned the work and whose departed husband, Donaes de Moor, was named in honor of the saint. In certain movements (including the Kyrie), Obrecht also deployed a second cantus-firmus melody: a Dutch song, *Gefft den armen gefangen* (Give to the Poor Prisoners), that calls on listeners to give alms, much as Adriane and Donaes are known to have done.

Obrecht's Kyrie follows the symmetrical and repetitive structure of the Mass text: three parts—Kyrie I, Christe, and Kyrie II—each with a threefold statement of the Latin words. Each of these three subsections in turn presents the cantus-firmus melodies in different combinations and musical contexts. It is interesting to consider how they align with each other, and how the cadential structure of the polyphonic ensemble relates to the cadence tones of the borrowed melodies. In Kyrie I the Latin melody appears in its usual place in the tenor and moving at its customary slow pace. Fifteenth- and sixteenth-century theorists would have argued that the mode of the tenor determines the melodic mode of the polyphonic ensemble. In this case, they seem to be one and the same, since Obrecht's polyphony for the Kyrie I centers around G, as does the plainsong.

The cadences of the polyphonic ensemble coincide with important places of articulation in the plainsong: they appear at the start of the tune (m. 6 in the transcription), just after the first phrase identifying the "blessed father" (m. 10), at the reference to St Donatian's name (m. 16), and at the conclusion of the tune (m. 27). The second of these cadences corresponds to another, more obscure quotation that Obrecht buried in his mass: in measures 10–11 the bassus part quotes the first seven notes of the bassus part of the *Missa Ecce ancilla Dominum* (Mass Behold the Handmaid of the Lord) by Johannes Ockeghem (ca. 1410–1497). It's unlikely that any but a trained musician would have caught the reference. Perhaps Obrecht meant to pay homage to Ockeghem (they met in 1484) as his own musical "father." The mass shares many stylistic features with Ockeghem, including his preference for artful counterpoint and florid melodies.

In the Christe the plainchant is transposed up to begin on D, and is placed so high in the tenor range that it actually sounds above the altus and superius (which sings quite low in its own range). The Latin cantus firmus is presented twice: once in a meter that is twice as slow as the other parts, then again at their pace. Such organizational schemes remind us of the old motet structures encountered in Ciconia and Du Fay (see Anthology 2 and 9), but they were part of the tenor-mass tradition, too. The cadences here center on G, just as they do in the other movements. But now the cantus firmus joins these as the fifth of the final sonorities (see mm. 46 and 58).

In Kyrie II the plainsong tenor returns to its original pitch. Now the Dutch song joins it, first in the altus part (stated twice, and each time also centered on G), then a third time in the bassus part (now centered on C). The chief effect of the latter transposition is that the cadential gestures heard in the upper voices in measures 89 and 96 are thwarted when the song moves up a whole tone to E. In the final phrase of the song, Obrecht alters the last note so that the borrowed melody permits the piece to close (m. 109).

The recording by the Cappella Pratensis features a realization of the entire musical mass in its correct liturgical sequence, including plainsong melodies of the Proper (that is, the texts of the Mass that vary according to the liturgical calendar) interspersed among Obrecht's polyphonic settings of the Ordinary (or fixed portions of the Mass text). There are also performances of each of the cantus-firmus melodies on their own. The group puts a premium on original sources and contexts. They sing from facsimiles of the original manuscripts, which are placed on a lectern before the choir (in this case an all-male ensemble, singing two to a part). The compact disc noted in our listening list also includes a reenactment of the mass filmed on location in Bruges. A companion website offers interactive analytical and cultural perspectives on the work and its context (see the listing of digital resources online).

7

JOHN DUNSTABLE (CA. 1390–1453)

Quam pulchra es

Motet, 1440–50

From John Dunstable, *Complete Works*, ed. Manfred Bukofzer, Musica Britannica, 8 (London: Stainer and Bell, 1970), pp. 112–13.

Quam pulchra es et quam decora, carissima in deliciis.	*How lovely and wonderful you are, most beloved, most sweet in your delights.*
Statura tua assimilata est palme, et ubera tua botris.	*Your stature is like a palm tree, and your breasts like a cluster of grapes.*
Caput tuum ut Carmelus, collum tuum sicut turris eburnea.	*Your head is like Mount Carmel, your neck like an ivory tower.*
Veni, dilecte me, egrediamur in agrum, et videamus si flores fructus parturierunt, si floruerunt mala Punica.	*Come, my love, let us go into the fields, and see if the flowers bear fruit and the pomegranates are in flower.*
Ibi dabo tibi ubera mea.	*There will I give you my breasts.*
Alleluia.	*Alleluia.*

The text of *Quam pulchra es* comes from the Old Testament Song of Songs, a collection of love poetry that often found its way into portions of the Christian liturgy. (See Anthology 20 and 21 for other works drawn from this source.) In the English liturgy of the fifteenth century, a plainsong melody with this text was used as a processional antiphon (a melody that framed the recitation of a psalm) for the Feast of the Blessed Virgin Mary. Some of John Dunstable's motets make use of that melody. This one does not, suggesting that the polyphony was conceived for voluntary devotions rather than as a part of the obligatory liturgy. In any case, to judge from its wide circulation in manuscripts produced on the European continent during the first half of the fifteenth century, *Quam pulchra es* was heard in contexts well beyond the official liturgy.

The devotional character of Dunstable's setting is confirmed by its musical style. He was certainly capable of composing elaborate pieces with carefully organized tenor melodies of the sort seen in Ciconia's *Doctorum principem* (Anthology 2) or Du Fay's *Supremum est mortalibus* (Anthology 9). This piece, however, is altogether more modest in its means. The uppermost line (cantus) is clearly the most important, tracing a beautiful arc of ascent, declamation, and then a rush of rhythmic energy as the music cadences at the end of each line of text. The cantus often moves in melodic thirds, with the result that it sounds remarkably modern and even triadic. The novelty of this sound was well recognized by fifteenth-century commentators.

The lower two voices support the cantus in a number of ways. They move in close rhythmic coordination with it, often declaiming the text at the same time. They also support it contrapuntally. Stressing a sonority long preferred by English composers of the fifteenth century, the tenor moves mainly in sixths and thirds with the cantus, then expands to an octave at each cadence (except for the cadence at "Punica" in m. 49, where they contract to a unison). The tenor–cantus duet, as in the case of *There is no rose* (Anthology 8), could be understood as musically self-sufficient. But Dunstable adds a contratenor to the mix. This voice part is of two minds, contrapuntally speaking. In some cadential passages it moves strictly in parallel with the cantus at a fourth below (mm. 12–14), thus creating sonorities that recall the improvisatory practices of faburden and other unwritten traditions of chant harmonization with which every chorister of the day was familiar. In other contexts the contratenor leaps about in sharp contrast to the other voices (and often below the tenor), hinting at an independent role and new musical range that composers of the mid-fifteenth century would be keen to explore.

Quam pulchra es is unusually declamatory, particularly since all three voices often join in rhythmic support of the repeated tones in the cantus part (at "carissima" in mm. 5–6, for instance). The contrast between this pleading recitation and the comparatively ornate rush to cadences makes for a tension that breaks through definitively at the climax of the piece, when two stark harmonies and an ensuing busy cadence (at the imploring command "Veni, dilecte me" in mm. 31–32) pierce a framing silence. The effect for modern listeners is poignant. To fifteenth-century ears it must have been equally striking: the cadence that immediately precedes the silence (at "eburnea") comes to rest on D. A cadence in this position is not usual in other compositions. But it is surprising in a piece centered on C, which in and of itself stands outside any of the accepted modal centers recognized by fifteenth-century music theorists. (Two more cadences to D echo the disruptive effect later in the piece.)

The move to D (and also to G in a previous phrase at "Carmelus") would have demanded quick thinking from Dunstable's singers. Unlike the cadences to C and F heard elsewhere in the piece, which can be performed as notated, those to G and D demand the insertion of temporary "false" tones (*musica ficta*) in the cantus part in order to sound correct. Modern editors suggest the implied F♯ and C♯ by placing accidentals above the staff. In practice, groups like the Hilliard Ensemble (as noted in our list of sound recordings) also inflect the contratenor part with *musica ficta* at many cadential points in order to avoid the harmonic interval of a tritone with the cantus line (listen, for instance, to mm. 17–18, 28–29, or 38). The result recalls the sound of a sort of cadential motion (called a "double-leading-tone cadence" by some modern musicologists) that had been around since the fourteenth century, and even before. Singing one to a part, the men of the Orlando Consort also sing with impeccable musical intonation and careful attention to the declamatory power of Dunstable's polyphony.

8

ANONYMOUS

There is no rose
Carol, early fifteenth century

From *Mediaeval Carols*, ed. John E. Stevens, 2nd rev. ed., Musica Britannica, 4 (London: Stainer and Bell, 1958), pp. 10–11. The text given below uses modern spellings.

There is no rose of such virtue
As is the rose that bore Jesus,
Alleluia.

For in this rose was contained
Both heaven and earth in a little space,
A thing to wonder at.

By that rose we may well see
That he is God in persons three,
But of equal form.

The angels sing to the shepherds,
"Glory in the highest to God."
Let us rejoice!

We leave behind this worldly mirth
And follow this joyful birth.
Let us go.

There is no rose survives in a two-voice polyphonic setting preserved in a parchment roll (*rotulus*) of the early fifteenth century. One of the most important sources for polyphonic English carols (popular religious songs), the roll is now housed at Trinity College, Cambridge. As in other carols of the day, each couplet of the text is punctuated by a refrain, or "burden," which is sung between each of the successive verses. Each of these in turn concludes with one in a series of exclamations. The subject matter suggests a Christmas pageant or procession. We know that monophonic carols were performed in this way, sometimes with room for the audience to join in for the refrain, while soloists took the intervening verses. The demands of the polyphonic notation suggest that *There is no rose* was sung by skilled choristers, perhaps at a church school or at the home of a wealthy patron.

The refrain is much more decorated than the melody for the couplets. It also refers obliquely to the body of the melody, since the final turn and cadence in the upper voice recall those of the second melodic phrase (at the words "that bore Jesus"). The connection provides a rounding effect, highlighting in sound the interplay of ideas in the two parts of the text, and "reminding" the singers to turn back to the refrain and then go on to the next part of the story. The overall form of the poem is also nicely embodied in the balanced succession of cadences: to G and then C in the refrain; to E and then twice to C in the verse.

The two notated voice parts in the Trinity College roll move in note-against-note counterpoint, chiefly in parallel sixths and thirds, sonorities favored by John Dunstable (see Anthology 7) and other English musicians in the mid-fifteenth century. The sound ideal of *There is no rose* thus contrasts with that of a work like Johannes Ciconia's *Doctorum principem* (Anthology 2), with its strong orientation around successions of fifths and octaves for important stresses. Cadences are formed with characteristic voice-leading: an octave or unison approached by its closest imperfect consonance, thus either a major sixth expanding to the octave, or a minor third contracting to a unison. This figure is further ornamented in the upper voice by a rhythmic repetition and downward melodic turn at the last instant, so that in several phrases the final tone is approached from below (and by a minor third).

The third phrase of the duet (mm. 15–16) offers a special type of cadence. Here the half step is in the descending rather than the ascending voice, and as such it creates a somewhat tentative closure recognized as exceptional even by musicians of the fifteenth and sixteenth centuries. In modern parlance, this is a Phrygian cadence, because of its association with modes centered on E. Renaissance theorists understood that cadences to E normally demanded this particular counterpoint, since their conception of musical space would not have allowed both F♯ and D♯ as tones available to form a cadence of the regular type in this position. Even the F♯ needed to form a regular cadence to G at the end of the first phrase of the piece stood outside the system of "real" music (*musica recta*). It was realized only in performance as unwritten, "false" or "imaginary" sound (*musica ficta*).

How have modern musicians approached the performance of this modest carol? An edition of the Trinity roll prepared by J. A. Fuller-Maitland and William Rockstro during the last decade of the nineteenth century adds a pair of vocal parts (bass and tenor) to the duet, as well as a keyboard accompaniment. The result often sounds more like a modern choral hymn than a fifteenth-century carol, with touches of tonal harmony and currents of imitative counterpoint. The more recent edition reproduced here (and used in the recording by the Oxford Camerata) realizes the carol in the manner of one of the improvisatory styles known variously as "sights" and "faburden." In the burden (refrain) some singers perform the pair of written lines, while others sing a third, unwritten line that moves in parallel fourths with the uppermost voice of the texture, forming the sweet harmonies typical of the English style. The men and women of the Oxford Camerata sing the opening (or burden) as a choir, with more than one singer to a part. The verses are performed one singer to a part.

9

GUILLAUME DU FAY (1397–1474)

Supremum est mortalibus
Motet, 1433

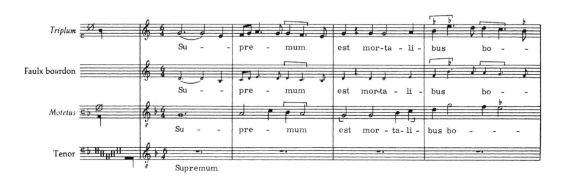

Triplum
Su - pre - mum est mor-ta - li - bus bo -

Faulx bourdon
Su - pre - mum est mor-ta - li - bus bo -

Motetus
Su - pre - mum est mor - ta-li - bus bo - - -

Tenor
Supremum

5
num Pax, o- pti - mum sum - mi de - i do - num.

num Pax, o-pti - mum sum - mi de - i do - num.

num Pax, o-pti - mum sum - mi de - i do - num.

11
Pa - ce ve - ro le - gem prae - stan-ti - a Vi - get at-que re -

Pa - ce ve - ro le - gem prae-stan-ti - - - - a Vi -

I,1   2   3   4   5

From Guillaume Dufay, *Opera Omnia*, ed. Heinrich Besseler, 6 vols., Corpus Mensurabilis Musicae, 1 (Rome: American Institute of Musicology, 1947–66), 1:59–63, with corrections of errors. Emended text and translation from Leofranc Holford-Strevens, "Du Fay the Poet? Problems in the Texts of his Motets," *Early Music History* 16 (1997): 97–160, at pp. 140–1; translation blended with Willem Elders, "Dufay's Concept of Faux-Bourdon," *Revue belge de musicologie* 43 (1989): 177–78.

Supremum est mortalibus bonum	The supreme good for mortals is
Pax, optimum summi dei donum.	Peace, the best gift of God the Highest.
Pace vero legum praestantia	In peacetime the rule of law
Viget atque recti constantia;	And the constancy of the right prevail.
Pace dies solutus et laetus,	In peacetime the day is free and happy,
Nocte somnus trahitur quietus;	At night quiet sleep is prolonged;
Pax docuit virginem ornare	Peace taught the maiden to adorn
Auro comam crinesque nodare;	Her hair with gold and to bind her tresses with a knot.
Pace rivi psallentes et aves	In peacetime the streams and the singing birds
Patent laeti collesque suaves	Are seen to rejoice and the pleasant hills.
Pace dives pervadit viator,	In peacetime the wealthy traveller reaches his destination,
Tutus arva incolit arator.	And the ploughman cultivates the fields in safety.
O sancta pax, diu expectata,	O holy peace, long awaited,
Mortalibus tam dulcis, tam grata,	So sweet and welcome to mortals,
Sis aeterna, firma, sine fraude,	Be eternal, firm, without deceit.
Fidem tecum semper esse gaude.	Rejoice that faith in you is everlasting.
Et qui nobis, o pax, te dedere	And may those, o peace, who gave thee to us
Possideant regnum sine fine:	possess their realms without end:
Sit noster hic pontifex aeternus	May our pope on earth be for ever
Eugenius et rex Sigismundus!	EUGENIUS AND OUR KING SIGISMUND.
Amen.	Amen.

TENOR

Pro pace, pro duobus magnis luminaribus mundi. Amen.	For peace, for the two great luminaries of the world. Amen.

Guillaume Du Fay's motet celebrated a peace treaty between his patron, Pope Eugenius IV, and King Sigismund of Hungary in the spring of 1433. This context is clearly reflected in the organization of the text of the motet, which unfolds in four clearly defined sections, each opening with an invocation of peace. Five couplets (each beginning with "peace") then spell out a long list of natural and human activities in which peace prevails. A further three couplets extol peace itself ("O holy peace"). The final couplet names the peacemakers, Eugenius and Sigismund.

Du Fay's music surrounds all of this with a well-ordered collage of sounds drawn from the traditions of sacred music. The piece is organized around a freely composed tenor melody that is heard twice—first in support of the litany of peaceful activities (mm. 11–52), then again for the praise of peace (mm. 56–97). Each statement of the tenor tune is organized into three presentations of the same slow-moving rhythm, one for each couplet of the main part of the Latin poem (compare the sequence of durations in mm. 11–25, 26–40, 41–55, 56–70, 71–85, and 86–100). In our modern edition, pairs of numerals indicate the tenor organization: Roman numbers mark the start of each statement of the rhythmic series, while Arabic numerals indicate the start of each statement of the melodic series.

This organizational technique is an old one: the fourteenth-century musician Egidius of Murino suggested that composers begin by putting the tones of the (borrowed) tenor in order before composing the upper voices. The same procedure can be heard in Johannes Ciconia's *Doctorum principem* (Anthology 2). The technique has been dubbed "isorhythm" in the modern critical literature, although musicians of the fourteenth and fifteenth centuries would not have recognized the term.

In many of his political motets, Du Fay extended this organizing principle to the upper voices, giving them identical melodic and rhythmic patterns that mirrored the structural divisions of the tenor. His approach in *Supremum est mortalibus* is subtler than this. The upper voices do not participate in the architecture of the tenor part, and so are free to form cadences in various places, not all of them important moments of repetition in the tenor plan itself.

Du Fay's tenor melody includes a brief quotation from a plainsong melody (mm. 101–106). *Isti sunt duae olivae* (These are two olives) comes from a feast in honor of Saints John and Paul. The idea must have been to draw positive comparisons between these saints and the modern dedicatees, whose names are sung in slow-moving chords right after the reference. There are also passages of improvised fauxbourdon heard during the introductory couplet (mm. 1–10), at the very end (110–13), and at the conclusion of some of the repeating tenor rhythmic segments (mm. 38–40 and 68–70).

The modern edition of *Supremum est mortalibus* seems to suggest that a fourth group of singers is needed for the fauxbourdon sections. But these improvised lines can just as easily be sung by those normally responsible for the tenor line, since that part is silent whenever Du Fay calls for fauxbourdon. The section of long notes (marked with fermatas in the modern edition) for the names of the dedicatees also raises questions for performers. It's possible simply to sing them as stark harmonies. The recording by the Clerks' Group takes the held notes (called "cantus coronatus" in theoretical writings of the fifteenth century) as invitations for florid improvisatory counterpoint. The performers have also made a careful study of the original manuscript sources of Du Fay's motet, judiciously adjusting the placement of text according to those documents, and making their own judgments about where to introduce *musica ficta*, the unwritten accidentals that were a fundamental part of the singer's craft during the fifteenth century.

Missa L'homme armé: Agnus Dei

Cantus-firmus mass, ca. 1450

From Guillaume Dufay, *Opera Omnia*, ed. Heinrich Besseler, 6 vols., Corpus Mensurabilis Musicae, 1 (Rome: American Institute of Musicology, 1947–66), 3:61–65. The tune shown on page 48 is taken from the mass; cf. also the version in Josquin's mass, Anthology 11, and the setting in Busnoys's mass, Example 5.2 in *Music in the Renaissance*.

(1) Canon: Cancer eat plenus sed redeat medius.

riddle culture

Agnus Dei, qui tollis peccata mundi: miserere nobis.	*Lamb of God, who takest away the sins of the world: have mercy on us.*
Agnus Dei, qui tollis peccata mundi: miserere nobis.	*Lamb of God, who takest away the sins of the world, have mercy on us.*
Agnus Dei, qui tollis peccata mundi: dona nobis pacem.	*Lamb of God, who takest away the sins of the world: give us peace.*

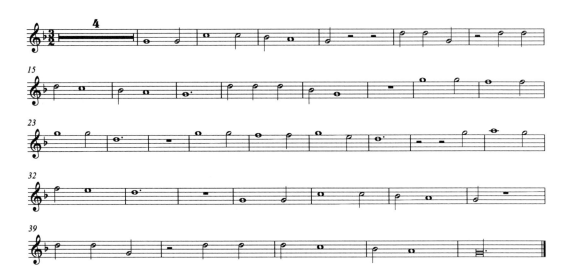

The *L'homme armé* (The Armed Man) tune first entered the repertory of polyphonic music in the middle years of the fifteenth century (see below, and also the discussion in chapter 5 of *Music in the Renaissance*). The recording by the Oxford Camerata includes a choral performance of the monophonic chanson on its own, as well as all five movements of Guillaume Du Fay's mass. This version of the tune uses B♭ throughout, just as Du Fay does in his presentation of the melody in his mass. Du Fay was not the first composer to treat it as the basis of a tenor mass—that distinction probably belongs to Antoine Busnoys. All sorts of explanations have been advanced for the tune's popularity with mass composers. As part of an emerging culture of homage and emulation, composers working in the *L'homme armé* tradition often showed a good deal of self-consciousness about the approaches their colleagues had taken. (For a section of a later setting by Josquin des Prez, see Anthology 11.)

In the case of mass movements like the Credo and Gloria, the repeating tenor cantus firmus gave composers a chance to organize long, digressive texts. The Kyrie and Agnus Dei movements, in contrast, have short texts, but ones that carry their own traditions of repetition and symmetry. Music can underscore these traditions in a variety of ways. In Du Fay's Agnus Dei, the conventional division of the Latin text into three symmetrically arranged sections mirrors the threefold repetitions of the phrase "Lamb of God." Agnus I and III are for four voices, with a slow-moving tenor. In Agnus II the tenor part is silent, and so Du Fay was able to write in the florid, contrapuntal style for three voices familiar from his secular compositions like *Par le regart* (Anthology 4). Meanwhile, the contratenor and bassus parts (in our edition they are called "contra" and "contrabassus") toss motives from the *L'homme armé* melody back and forth as the section draws to a close.

In Agnus III (starting at m. 75), the tenor returns in its familiar structural role and at its previous pace. In order to perform the part correctly, Du Fay's singers needed to decipher a cryptic Latin canon, or "rule": "Cancer eat plenus sed redeat medius" (Let the crab go forward whole, but return half). Properly decoded, the canon instructs the singers to perform the notes of the *L'homme armé* tune first in the notated values but in reverse order, then in the correct sequence but at twice the speed.

It is interesting to note the varied ways in which Du Fay treats the tenor at cadential articulations. In some contexts the tenor serves as the foundation of the cadence, approaching an octave through the closest imperfect consonance according to fifteenth-century contrapuntal norms. This often happens in coordination with the beginnings and endings of tenor phrases, so that the cadences serve to make the tenor tune audible, even when it moves very slowly (see mm. 5, 13, and 39). In other contexts Du Fay seems to build counterpoint *despite* the tenor phrasing, as in measures 22–29, when the **b** phrase of the *L'homme armé* tune is presented. (Although this, too, is subject to context, as we can hear in m. 125 of Agnus III, when the **b** phrase of the tenor ends as the foundation of a strong cadence to D, just before the last gesture of the entire work.)

Finally, we should note the important contrapuntal role played by the bassus. As its name suggests, it often occupies a range below that of the tenor. Thus it both extends the overall polyphonic range of the ensemble and serves what sounds like a surprisingly modern (even harmonic) role in cadences, leaping up a fourth to the final tone of the phrase. This sound would become the norm after 1500 in the music of Josquin and his contemporaries.

Missa L'homme armé super voces musicales: Kyrie

Cantus-firmus mass, ca. 1490–95

From Josquin des Prez, *Opera Omnia*, ed. A. Smijers (Amsterdam: G. Alsbach & Co., 1957), 1/i:1–5. The tune shown on page 55 is taken from the mass; cf. also the version in Du Fay's mass, Anthology 10, and the setting in Busnoys's mass, Example 5.2 in *Music in the Renaissance*.

Kyrie eleison.   *Lord have mercy.*
Christe eleison.   *Christ have mercy.*
Kyrie eleison.   *Lord have mercy.*

The *Missa L'homme armé super voces musicales* (Armed Man Mass upon Musical Syllables) is one of two tenor cantus-firmus masses Josquin des Prez composed based on a famous secular tune. The mass is preserved in a manuscript made for the Papal Chapel about 1495, quite possibly while Josquin himself was a member of the pope's musical household. In 1502 Ottaviano Petrucci gave it pride of place in a new series of mass prints devoted exclusively to works by Josquin.

As in Du Fay's *Missa L'homme armé* (Anthology 10), the tune appears in Josquin's mass in each of the five fixed movements of the Ordinary: Kyrie, Gloria, Credo, Sanctus, and Agnus Dei. But Josquin literally took things several steps further, as the cantus firmus is heard in succession beginning on each of the six solmization syllables of the hexachordal system. (It occurs twice in the Agnus Dei.) In the Kyrie, the *L'homme armé* melody begins on C (*ut*). Josquin mapped the symmetrical refrain form implicit in the tune (**Abb′A**) onto the symmetrical design of the Mass section itself: the **A** phrase corresponds to Kyrie I (mm. 1–18), the twin **b** phrases to Christe (mm. 19–62), and the reprise of the **A** phrase to Kyrie II (mm. 63–87).

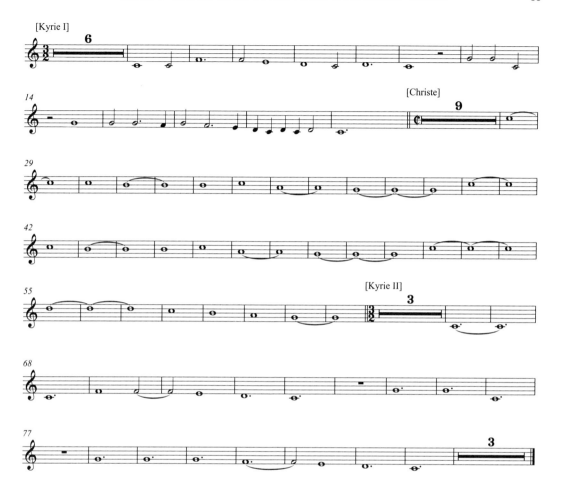

While the slow-moving tenor controls the pitches available for use in the other parts, it does not determine the major cadences (or, therefore, the overall modality) of the movement. The *L'homme armé* tune cadences (in this transposition) to C, then G, then C, for instance, whereas the corresponding cadences in Josquin's polyphony are to A (Kyrie I), E (Christe), and D (Kyrie II). In the last case, Josquin's tenor concludes three measures before the end of the movement as a whole. In this way the mass remains centered on D, even though the cantus firmus cycles through the entire hexachord. Solmization and modality, Josquin seems to remind us, are not the same thing.

Josquin's Kyrie is also notable for the ways in which the outer voices occasionally anticipate and echo the melodic profile of the tenor tune, even as they make lively counterpoint with each other. This procedure, too, has a systematic quality: in Kyrie I it is the superius that anticipates the tune (mm. 2–8); in Christe it moves down to the altus part (mm. 20–27);

and in Kyrie II it finally reaches the bassus (mm. 64–70). We should also note the tight, sequential motives drawn from the tune that are heard in the superius in measures 41–50 of Christe, similar to the motivic writing in Josquin's *Ave Maria . . . virgo serena* (Anthology 14). This kind of imitative complexity, scholars have argued, is a hallmark of Josquin's style. He was certainly not the only composer to write this way, but he is justly famous for it. The men and women of the Tallis Scholars (see our list of recordings) are especially adept at bringing out the independence of the various lines, which ebb and flow with great beauty and subtlety in their recording.

JOHN WILBYE (1574–1638)

Draw on, sweet Night

Madrigal, 1609

From *The Oxford Book of English Madrigals*, ed. Philip Ledger (London and New York: Oxford University Press, 1978), pp. 76–90.

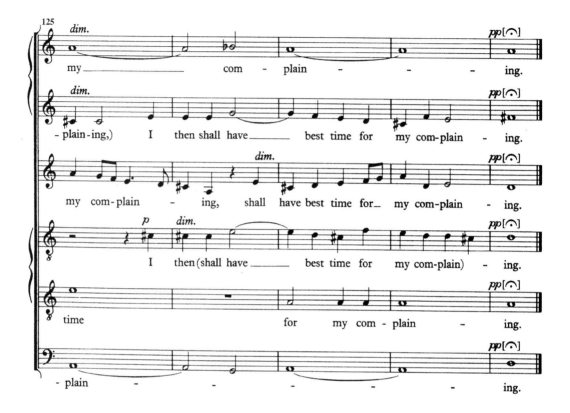

Draw on, sweet Night, best friend unto those cares
That do arise from painful melancholy.
My life so ill through want of comfort fares,
That unto thee I consecrate it wholly.

Sweet Night, draw on! My griefs, when they be told
To shades and darkness, find some ease from paining.
And while thou all in silence dost enfold,
I then shall have best time for my complaining.

John Wilbye spent much of his career as a domestic musician in the service of the wealthy Kytson family, both in their London home and in their country residence. One of Wilbye's madrigals appeared in the famous collection *The Triumphes of Oriana* (1601), prepared by Thomas Morley in honor of Queen Elizabeth I. He wrote in a wide range of genres, from light four-voice canzonettes to more serious multivoice compositions like this one, which was published in his *Second Set of Madrigales* of 1609. The book was dedicated to Lady Arabella Stuart, a niece of one of Wilbye's other protectors, Sir Charles Cavendish.

   Draw on, sweet Night, considered by some among the finest madrigals of its day, offers a musical landscape of richly contrasting ideas. In the poem, the speaker looks forward to night as a release from "painful melancholy." The idea seems simple enough. But the conclusion of the text is less hopeful than we might have expected: night provides a forum for continued complaints, not a respite from them. The varied reprise of the opening line at the center of the poem is revealing: the reordering of the words ("Sweet Night, draw on," rather than "Draw on, sweet Night") hints at the change of mood from hope to obsession, as the musical setting returns to mull over the opening motives no less than the words they set.

Wilbye's response to this material, too, is more complex than we might first think. Perhaps the most notable moment of the piece comes at the poetic reprise, where the echo of the opening lines is joined by a musical reprise of material drawn from the opening of the piece (mm. 51–70). But just as the words are slightly rearranged, so too is the music: the melodic figure from the cantus part at the opening is now heard in the tenor, a musical "inversion" of the contrapuntal texture that nicely mirrors the poetic inversion of the word order.

The two large musical sections that correspond to "Draw on, sweet Night" and "Sweet Night, draw on" both include a remarkable gesture of interruption. Following a long build-up of crushing suspended dissonances at "painful melancholy" in the first section of the piece, the altus and quintus voices at last seem ready to resolve to a cadence on D in measure 31. But that's not what we hear: the texture suddenly changes, with the altus and quintus left hanging in midair, and although the tenor sounds out the missing tone, the musical fabric is by this point quite different as we move on to a new line of text ("My life so ill through want of comfort fares"). As in Marenzio's *Liquide perle* (Anthology 1), the new texture also explores new tonal registers, trading the "hard" F♯s and C♯s (each solmized as *mi*) of the previous section for "soft" F♮s and B♭s (solmized as *fa*). It is an extreme contrast of sonority that would have struck listeners of the day as jarring and poignant.

The second statement of "Sweet Night, draw on" also culminates in an unsettling effect. The texture builds, pointing toward a temporary resting point on D. Then, in measures 65–70, Wilbye pauses and repeats the musical idea as a distant (remembered?) echo, trading C♯s in one of the tenor voice parts (m. 67) for C♮s in the other tenor voice part (m. 68), which then traces a mournful linear descent beneath the other parts (mm. 68–70). This is the "tear motive" heard in pieces like John Dowland's *Flow my tears* and *Mille regrets*, commonly attributed to Josquin des Prez (Anthology 15). The gesture may in the case of Wilbye's piece also point back to a moment in the bassus voice ("through want of comfort fares") that traced a similar linear descent, this time ending with a touching Phrygian cadence to A (mm. 38–39). This same melodic figure serves as the final gesture of the piece (bassus, mm. 124–25). It seems unlikely that the obsessive pain of this speaker will stop any time soon.

This moving work has been recorded frequently and by different ensembles, each with different effect. The Tallis Scholars render the madrigal as a true chamber piece, with one singer to a voice part and many affective pauses and dynamic swells. The Sarum Consort features one or two singers to a part, but also adds lute accompaniment (by Jacob Heringman, the same performer featured in Dentice's Fantasia, Anthology 25) in support of the singers, and with discrete ornamentation according to the principles of diminution that we explore in *Music in the Renaissance*. The recording by the Hilliard Ensemble features an all-male ensemble and period pronunciation of the text. It is an especially effective presentation of the madrigal. The dynamic and expressive markings in our edition are the work of a modern editor, and do not appear in the original source.

BARTOLOMEO TROMBONCINO (1470–1534)

Ostinato vo' seguire

Frottola, before 1508

Edited by Richard Freedman. Modern edition prepared from *Frottole libro nono* (Venice: Ottaviano Petrucci, 1508–1509), fols. 12ᵛ–13ʳ

Ostinato vo' seguire   *a*   *I shall resolutely follow*
La magnanima mia impresa.   *b*   *My magnanimous enterprise.*
Fame, Amor qual voi offesa,   *b*   *Love, do me what offense you will,*
S'io dovessi ben morire   *a*   *If I were indeed to die*
    Ostinato vo' seguire   *A*   *I shall resolutely follow*
    La magnanima mia impresa.   *B*   *My magnanimous enterprise.*

Fame, ciel, fame, Fortuna   *c*   *Do me, Heaven, do me, Fortune,*
Bene o mal como a te piace   *d*   *Good or ill as you please,*
Né piacer né ingiuria alcuna   *c*   *Neither pleasure nor pain*
Per avilirmi o far più audace   *d*   *Will weaken me nor make me bolder,*
Ché de l'un non son capace   *d*   *For I am not capable of the first,*
L'altro più non po fugire.   *a*   *And the other I cannot escape.*
    Ostinato vo' seguire   *A*   *I shall resolutely follow*
    La magnanima mia impresa.   *B*   *My magnanimous enterprise.*

Vinca o perda, io non attendo   *c*   *Win or lose, I do not expect*
De mia impresa altro che honore   *d*   *From my undertaking other than honor;*
Sopra il ciel beato ascendo;   *c*   *Over blessed heaven I rise.*
S'io ne resto vincitore   *d*   *If I do not remain the victor,*
S'io la perdo al fin gran core   *d*   *If I fail it, in the end a great heart*
Mostrarà l'alto desire.   *a*   *Will show my great desire.*
    Ostinato vo' seguire   *A*   *I shall resolutely follow*
    La magnanima mia impresa.   *B*   *My magnanimous enterprise.*

Bartolomeo Tromboncino was among the most important composers of frottole, a generic term for a variety of Italian polyphonic songs cultivated in courtly and amateur circles during the late fifteenth and early sixteenth centuries. Tromboncino was active mainly at the court of Isabella d'Este in Mantua, where she moved from her native Ferrara following her marriage to a Gonzaga prince. Frottole were the work of poet-improvisers, many of whom accompanied themselves on lute or lira da braccio (a bowed instrument held to the chest). Some of these works eventually found their way into print, most notably in the 11 books of frottole issued by the pioneering Venetian music printer Ottaviano Petrucci between 1504 and 1514.

Ostinato vo' sequire comes from Book 9 of this series, published in 1508–1509. This version, like the others in Petrucci's main series, is set for four polyphonic voices. But in 1509 Petrucci also issued a book by a lutenist, Franciscus Bossinensis, in which this and other frottole were arranged for solo voice and lute accompaniment. (The altus was omitted. Tenor and bassus parts were combined in lute tablature; the cantus line was for the vocalist. This is the version presented in the recording by the ensemble Circa 1500.) Presumably, this collection was for amateurs who wanted to accompany themselves as they sang. Bossinensis also offered a number of instrumental pieces in his collection, each linked to the various frottole with which it shared a modal center. Perhaps the idea was to introduce the song with a kind of instrumental prelude.

Petrucci's books of frottole embraced a wide range of poetic forms and types, each with its special refrain schemes and meters. *Ostinato vo' seguire* is a barzeletta, one of the most common types in the repertory. It consists of rhymed lines of eight syllables that unfold according to a stereotypical plan: a refrain (*ripresa*) of four lines (**abba**); a succession of verses (*mutazioni*), each with two couplets rhyming **cdcd**; and a two-line *volta* (rhyming **da**) that turns back to the rhyme of the refrain, which then repeats in abbreviated form (just two lines). This poetic design (indicated by lowercase letters) is joined with two musical sections (uppercase letters), as follows:

[*ripresa*]	[*mutazioni*]	[*volta*]
ab ba	**cd cd**	**da**
A B	**A A**	**B**

The **A** section (mm. 1–8) is quite short, while the **B** section (mm. 9–31) is much more expansive. A coda (mm. 32–46) rounds out the work.

Tromboncino's music for these lyrics closely mirrors the form of the poetry: each line gets its own melodic phrase. Like the paired couplets, the melodic ideas seem to come in sharply profiled pairs. In the refrain, for instance, the first phrase begins with an emphatic recitation on G, then falls quickly to pause on D (mm. 1–4). The second phrase makes up for lost time, starting with an energetic octave descent from high G to low G, then returning to a syncopated cadence on C (mm. 5–8). Subsequent phrases elaborate these two contrasting ideas, punctuating each end-rhyme with a cadence to C or a pause on D or B♮. The coda lacks the paired periodic design just heard. But it draws out a final burst of contrapuntal energy before letting the lower parts have the last word (mm. 42–46).

The lower voices support this melodic design in a number of elementary ways. The cantus and tenor form the structural duet found throughout polyphonic music of the period, generally moving in parallel thirds and sixths, except at cadences, where they move out to a stable octave. The bassus part sounds to modern ears as if it is providing the "root" of triads heard above. In fact, Tromboncino and his contemporaries had no such concept of invertible triads. The approach here followed a different kind of intervallic thinking: the bassus part simply forms alternating fifths and thirds with the main tones of the melody, a technique that long remained a part of improvisatory practice in the fifteenth and sixteenth centuries.

The extent to which a strophic setting of a poem (with the same music for each stanza) can attend to the meaning of individual words is by definition limited. But Tromboncino's music nevertheless marks the themes of the poem in important ways. For example, the stubborn repetition of G at "ostinato" seems to say, "I'm so resolute that I'll stick with this single note." Elsewhere the contour of the vocal line is very florid, with decorated runs highlighting "magnanimity" (from the Latin meaning "greatness of spirit").

The coda draws these two contradictory musical and rhetorical stances together one last time—at first reciting resolutely, then wildly insisting on the "nobility" of the speaker's enterprise. As the various stanzas explain, "neither pleasure nor pain" will change his resolve. Fortune has its reasons, but what matters to the persona imagined by this poem is that regardless of the outcome, he will have found "honor" and "a great desire." The strategic placement of these ideas at the ends of lines means that they, too, will be marked off with grandiose vocal flourishes.

Ave Maria . . . virgo serena

Motet, ca. 1480

From *Anthology of Renaissance Music*, ed. Allan Atlas (New York: W. W. Norton & Company, 1998), pp. 159–65. Used by permission of Alejandro Enrique Planchart.

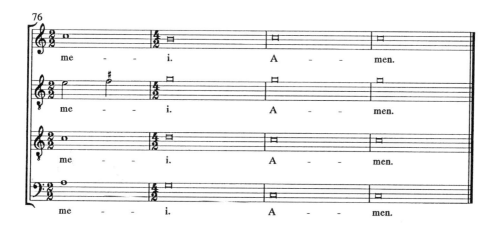

Ave Maria, gratia plena	*Hail Mary, full of grace,*
Dominus tecum, virgo serena.	*The Lord is with you, serene Virgin.*
Ave, cuius conceptio	*Hail whose conception,*
Solemni plena gaudio,	*Full of solemn rejoicing,*
Caelestia, terrestria	*Fills heaven and earth*
Nova replet laetitia.	*With new joy.*
Ave, cuius nativitas	*Hail whose nativity*
Nostra fuit solemnitas,	*Gave us solemnity,*
Ut lucifer, lux oriens,	*As the light of the morning star*
Verum solem praeveniens.	*Precedes the true sun.*
Ave, pia humilitas,	*Hail, pious humility,*
Sine viro fecunditas,	*Without a man made fruitful,*
Cuius annunciatio	*Whose annunciation*
Nostra fuit salvatio.	*Gave us salvation.*
Ave, vera virginitas,	*Hail, true virginity,*
Immaculata castitas,	*Immaculate chastity,*
Cuius purificatio	*Whose purification*
Nostra fuit purgatio.	*Purged our sins.*
Ave, praeclara omnibus	*Hail, foremost in all*
Angelicis virtutibus,	*Angelic virtues,*
Cuius fuit assumptio	*Whose assumption*
Nostra glorificatio.	*Was our glorification.*
O mater Dei,	*O Mother of God,*
Memento mei.	*remember me.*
Amen.	*Amen.*

Ave Maria . . . virgo serena has long been one of Josquin des Prez's most famous compositions. The motet probably dates from the early 1480s, since it is preserved in a manuscript copied at the imperial court at Innsbruck about this time. Exactly where or why Josquin wrote it is uncertain, but *Ave Maria . . . virgo serena* occupies an important place in the story of his music and of changing styles in the late fifteenth century.

The opening of the text of the motet derives from an old Marian prayer, representing a tradition of devotional music directed toward Mary's intercessory powers that emerged with special force during the fifteenth century. It then moves to a series of four-line stanzas, each made up of rhymed couplets, that recall in turn the most important moments in Mary's life: her conception, her birth, the annunciation of her role in a divine plan, her purification, and her assumption into heaven. These correspond to the five major Marian feasts of the liturgical year. The motet closes with a personal prayer (turning from the collective voice to the singular) that was apparently added for this setting. It does not figure in the original prayer, although the same personal supplication was known in northern France, attached to devotional images and other motets, as we can hear, for example, in William Byrd's *Ave verum corpus* (Anthology 19). Whether the "me" mentioned in the last section of the poem was meant to be a particular petitioner or the singers in general we cannot say.

Josquin's response to this text mirrors the overall form just described. Contrasting textures, meters, and points of arrival mark out the introductory frame, each of the four-line "remembrances," and the closing prayer. Three techniques in particular call for comment: the use of imitative counterpoint as a structural procedure, the palpable sense of dynamic growth and development in the musical lines, and the emphasis on varied means of making the text intelligible and enhancing its meaning.

The new structural role for imitative counterpoint is prominent from the outset. Brief passages of imitative writing are present in earlier works like Johannes Ciconia's *Doctorum principem* (at the echoing statements of Francesco Zabarella's name; Anthology 2) and Antoine Busnoys's *Ja que li ne s'i attende* (buried in the **b** section of the song; Anthology 5). In Josquin's motet each line of the prayer gets its own melodic profile, which is systematically imitated in each voice part in succession. The end of one point of imitation (as such thematic expositions are called) neatly folds into the beginning of the next, creating a seamless texture that at last draws to a coordinated cadence in measure 30, as the cantus and altus approach octave Cs by way of the closest imperfect consonance.

This cadence followed a long-established convention. Indeed, the same characteristic approach to the same cadential tone can be heard at the end of other sections of *Ave Maria . . . virgo serena* (at "laetitia" in m. 27, "praeveniens" in m. 39, and "purgatio" in m. 55). The imitative ideal has effectively erased the old hierarchical relationship among the various voice roles, which are now equal in their lyricism and level of rhythmic activity. This new functional equivalence also has the effect of expanding the vocal range, particularly as the parts often imitate each other at the octave.

Josquin treats subsequent sections of the text with an impressive array of other musical textures. There are imitative duets (mm. 28–33 are especially beautiful), as well as passages in which pairs of voices declaim the text more or less simultaneously (mm. 39–47). There are extended passages of homorhythmic writing in the triple-meter section starting at measure 47 and in the closing personal prayer starting at measure 73. There are even hints of the old cantus-firmus technique, here reconfigured so that the superius seems to float in comparatively slow-moving tones above the rest of the voices (in the superius part starting at m. 64).

This last passage, like a number of others in the motet, may reflect Josquin's attempt to represent the ideas described in the text. Hovering above the texture as it does, the superius part seems to express the theological point made in the text: Mary's assumption into heaven.

This same tendency to "paint" the text can be heard in the sequential ascent in measures 23–27 that underscores the way in which Mary's own conception fills "heaven and earth with new joy." For all these reasons, Josquin's *Ave Maria . . . virgo serena* deserves its prominent place in our image of Renaissance music. Unlike some other sacred and secular pieces of the fifteenth century, it presents no special problems of text placement: Josquin's lines are crafted in such a declamatory way that it seems almost self-evident. The very clarity and seeming simplicity of the style, however, are precisely what makes it challenging to perform. The Hilliard Ensemble (an all-male group, singing one to a part) and a group simply called Alamire (a mixed group of men and women, with more than one to a part) do an especially effective job of balancing the declamatory moments with the contrapuntal movement that surrounds them.

JOSQUIN DES PREZ (?) (CA. 1450–1521)

Mille regrets

Chanson, Before 1533

From *The Oxford Book of French Chansons*, ed. Frank Dobbins (Oxford: Oxford University Press, 1987), pp. 1–3.

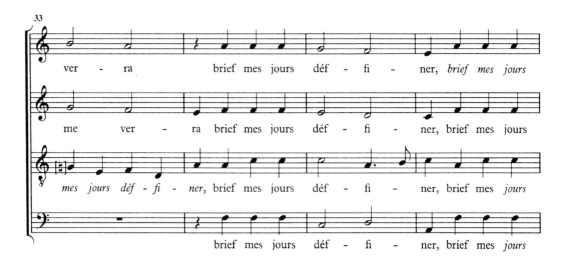

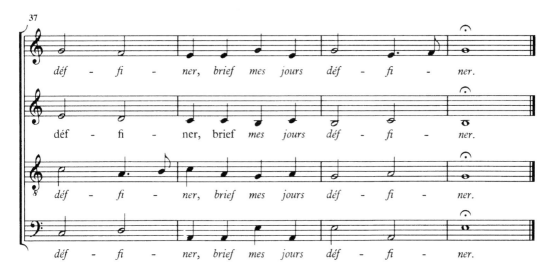

Mille regrets de vous abandonner
Et d'élonger votre face amoureuse;
J'ai si grand dueil et peine douloureuse
Qu'on me verra brief mes jours déffiner.

A thousand regrets in leaving you,
And in losing sight of your loving look;
I have such great sorrow and sad pain
That one can see how my days are numbered.

The text of this famous chanson draws on a tradition of serious poetry that was fashionable at French-speaking courts around 1500. Music books of the day include little clusters of pieces on the "regrets" theme by Loyset Compère, Pierre de La Rue, Hayne van Ghizeghem, and others. Josquin des Prez took part in this tradition, too, although his authorship of this chanson is no longer considered certain. There is no early manuscript or printed source that can be traced to Josquin's orbit, and *Mille regrets* seems quite unlike the chansons for which Josquin's authorship is unassailable. It is nevertheless very beautiful, and remains a frequently recorded and performed work. It survives not only in a version for four voices, but also in a number of instrumental arrangements from the middle years of the sixteenth century. Many of these have been recorded and are listed in the online materials.

Like many other "regrets" poems, this text obsessively worries over lost love, even to the point of physical suffering. In many ways the speaker shows all the hallmarks of erotic melancholy, a condition repeatedly explored in the literature and music of the sixteenth century. For all the pain and urgency, however, the speaker has formed his thoughts in a surprisingly coherent way: four lines of ten-syllable verse, all aligned in a neatly balanced rhyme scheme (**abba**). The symmetrical organization extends to the main division of ideas. Lines 1 and 2 recount the beloved's absence, while lines 3 and 4 speak of current suffering and the escape that won't come soon enough.

The composer of *Mille regrets* was careful to join each line with a distinctive melodic phrase in the conventional way. The chanson is unusual, however, in the extent to which it avoids solid cadences. Indeed, we'll be more frustrated than satisfied if we listen for the customary contrapuntal motion expanding outward to an octave (from a major sixth) or contracting to a unison (from a minor third) at the ends of poetic lines. (See, for example, the two contrapuntal duets at "peine douloureuse," mm. 19–24.) Even the ending is equivocal: where is the contrapuntal motion from D to E that ought to balance the descent in the superius part from F to E in mm. 37–38? The coda (mm. 38–39) dissipates musical energy as the voices rock between sonorities built on A and E. This sort of "plagal" motion (so named because of its association with the plagal forms of the Renaissance modes) is one of a number of typical closing formulas available to sixteenth-century composers. We hear it again in pieces by Janequin (Anthology 16), Arcadelt (Anthology 17), Byrd (Anthology 19), Lhéritier (Anthology 20), Palestrina (Anthology 21), Tallis (Anthology 22), Dentice (Anthology 25), and Gesualdo (Anthology 27).

Such ambiguity is a characteristic feature of works centered around the tone E. As we saw in the commentary to *There is no rose* (Anthology 8), cadences to this tone are formed with contrapuntal motion that is different from that used in all the other customary steps of Renaissance musical parlance. Cadences to E, or temporary cadences to other tones using the so-called Phrygian cadence, were often used by fifteenth- and sixteenth-century composers as markers of emotional distress, longing, or unfinished business. This set of associations perfectly suits the subject matter of *Mille regrets*.

This insight enables us to hear the avoided, tentative cadences of *Mille regrets* in new ways. The strong melodic profile of the descending scale segment A, G, F, E or E, D, C, B (the "tear motive" or "Phrygian tetrachord") emerges as the musical marker of an obsessive fixation that never quite resolves itself. It is first heard in the middle of the musical texture at "Et d'élonger" (altus, mm. 7–9, 10–12), each time harmonized with a lower part (bassus, then tenor) that makes a succession of thirds and fifths with it. The result reminds of us of the romanesca bass line used so often by improvisers of the day. (A related pattern occurs in Diego Ortiz's *Recercada ottava*, Anthology 24.) The tetrachord rapidly emerges from this hidden space to sound out at the extremes of the texture: in the superius (mm. 13–15, again with the romanesca bass) and at last in the bassus (mm. 15–17), where it creates the characteristically inconclusive Phrygian cadence with the tenor part in a cascade of sound that recalls another unwritten tradition, fauxbourdon, which we have encountered in works like *There is no rose* (Anthology 8) and Du Fay's *Supremum est mortalibus* (Anthology 9). In this practice, two written voices moving generally in parallel sixths are joined by a third unwritten part that shadows the upper of the pair at a fourth below.

The descending tetrachord and its tentative cadence come at a crucial moment in the text, just where memory of a "loving face" is most powerfully felt. It hardly seems coincidental that this same descending tetrachord (again with its romanesca bass line) returns in the last line of the chanson (at "brief mes jours déffiner"). In case we have forgotten, the music reminds us that the memory of loss and the urge to flee from life are inextricably linked. *Mille regrets* thus joins a long line of compositions that express in sound the condition of the melancholy lover. (For more on this theme, see the commentary to Wilbye's *Draw on, sweet Night*, Anthology 12.)

Martin menoit

Chanson, 1535

From Clément Janequin, *Chansons polyphoniques*, ed. A. Tillman Merritt and François Lesure, 6 vols. (Monaco: Editions de L'Oiseau-Lyre, 1965), 2:155–60.

Martin menoit son pourceau au marché	*Martin was taking his pig to market*
Avec Alix qui en la plaine grande	*With Alice, who when right in the open*
Pria Martin de faire le péché	*Begged Martin to commit the sin*
De l'ung sur l'aultre, et Martin luy demande:	*Of lying one with another, but Martin asked:*
"Et qui tiendroit nostre pourceau, friande?"	*"And who will hold onto our pig, my dear?"*
"Qui," dist Alix, "bon remede il y a."	*To which Alice replied, "There's an easy solution."*
Lors le pourceau a sa jambe lya	*Then she tied the piglet to her leg.*
Et Martin juche qui lourdement engaine	*But when Martin mounted and was heavily engaged*
Le porc eut peur et Alix s'escria:	*The pig took fright and Alice cried:*
"Serre Martin, nostre pourceau m'entraine."	*"Push, Martin, our piglet is dragging me off."*

Clément Janequin is famous for his long, programmatic chansons, in which imitation of the sounds of birds, battle, and even street cries are worked out in musical counterpoint. In this piece, first published by Pierre Attaingnant in 1535, we can hear similar attempts to represent the events and sounds imagined by the text. Janequin's piece was widely published and republished during the sixteenth century. After the initial appearance in Attaingnant's chansonnier of 1535, it was reissued in collections brought out in Venice (by Gardane), in Lyons (by Moderne), and in Paris (by Du Chemin). Several transcriptions for lute also survive (some of these have been recorded, as listed in our online index of recommended sound recordings). Considered in the context of the flowing lyricism that we often associate with the French chanson of the mid-sixteenth century (in the music of Claudin de Sermisy, for instance), this work represents some very different stylistic (no less than literary) trends.

Many French chansons are notable for their balanced, careful coordination of rhyme and cadence. *Martin menoit* begins by mapping rhyme and phrase: the first main cadence to G in measure 7 comes with the end of verse 1, the second to B♭ in measure 12 with the end of verse 2. The counterpoint is rhythmically busy, but in fact consists mainly of some basic elements familiar from other chansons of the middle years of the sixteenth century. The superius and tenor often move in lightly ornamented parallel sixths before converging on a syncopated cadence. This technique is at the heart of the lyrical French chanson as heard in the works of composers like Janequin's contemporary Claudin de Sermisy.

Elsewhere in this piece we hear closely spaced imitative duets between different combinations of voices. In the hands of some chanson composers, such counterpoint could approach the slow and serious pace of a motet. But that is certainly not Janequin's approach here. Indeed, the most striking thing about Janequin's setting is the way in which the musical fabric follows the sense of the text by the French court poet Clément Marot, especially the various bits of speech quoted there. For instance, what is prepared as a cadence to mark the end of verse 3 (to B♭ in m. 16) is undercut by the tenor, which starts the next line of text already in measure 15, no doubt to highlight the continuation of a single thought that runs into the next line of the poem ("to commit the sin of lying one with another"). A plagal cadence to D in measure 20 frames Martin's worried question, which itself is promptly interrupted (in mm. 24–25) by

Alice's emphatic response (now at last the superius joins in). The definitive cadence to D at the end of her "easy solution" is clue enough to her assured manner. We can almost hear the ensemble imitate their voices: the three lowest voices for Martin's question (see m. 21), then a piercing entry by the superius in the approach to the cadence (in mm. 26–28).

Still elsewhere, Janequin's music conjures the gestures and images of the poem. In measures 30–32, for example, the superius makes a series of dissonant suspensions with the lower voices in an apt representation of the knot that Alice makes to "tie" the pig to her leg. As Martin mounts her (mm. 32–35 and 35–38), the same melodic idea climbs upward from the bassus through the tenor, altus, and superius in turn. Perhaps most interesting of all are the ways in which Janequin's music works to manifest the sounds of Marot's world, especially Alice's cries (starting with "Push, Martin" in m. 42) as the panicked pig takes off. Janequin's music seems to pick up where verbal language breaks down.

The Ensemble Clément Janequin has great fun with the piece, taking pains to bring out the dialogue, the crude exclamations, and the frenetic energy of the scene. The singers perfectly capture the spirit of the composition, including a somewhat exaggerated "plagal" cadence at the end (mm. 56–57), in which the final sonority on G is approached from one built on C. The effect is to drag things out, just as Alice feels herself dragged away by the pig. (We also encounter this type of cadence, although with different expressive effect, in *Mille regrets* and many other pieces listed in the commentary to Anthology 15.) We should also note that the *musica ficta* E♭s suggested by the modern editors in this concluding passage of Janequin's chanson are made necessary by the counterpoint in measure 55, which requires an E♭ in the bassus (and then the altus) in order to avoid melodic and harmonic tritones with the B♭s that appear in those voice parts.

JACQUES ARCADELT (?1507–1568)

Il bianco e dolce cigno

Madrigal, before 1538

From Jacques Arcadelt, *Opera Omnia*, ed. Albert Seay, vol. 2, *Madrigali: Libro primo*, Corpus Mensurabilis musicae, 31 (Rome: American Institute of Musicology, 1965), pp. 38–40.

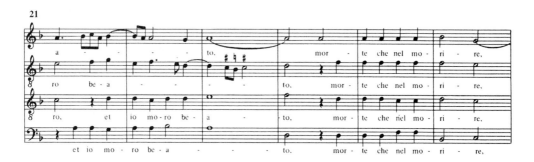

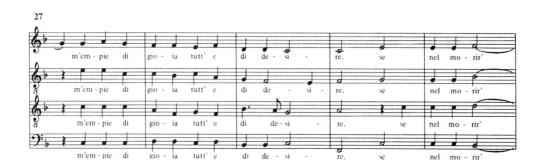

Il bianco e dolce cigno	*The white and gentle swan*
cantando more. Et io	*dies singing. And I,*
piangendo giung' al fin del viver mio.	*weeping, approach the end of my life.*
Stran' e diversa sorte,	*Strange and different fate,*
ch'ei more sconsolato	*that he dies disconsolate*
et io moro beato.	*and I die happy.*
Morte che nel morire	*Death that in dying*
m'empie di gioia tutt' e di desire.	*fills me with complete joy and desire.*
Se nel morir' altro dolor non sento	*If in dying I feel no other sorrow,*
di mille mort' il dì sarei contento.	*A thousand deaths a day would content me.*

Jacques Arcadelt's *Il bianco e dolce cigno* was already famous in its own day; indeed, it is perhaps the most popular madrigal of the sixteenth century. First published in 1538, it was still in print over a century later. The music is finely tuned to the imagery, form, and syntax of the poem. Arcadelt manages this feat by fragmenting and reinterpreting the text in ways that might not occur to us when reading it on the page. The text is poised at the intersection of two "deaths": the "disconsolate" death of the swan and the blissful one that the speaker is willing to endure a thousand times a day. Considered against the backdrop of sixteenth-century literary tastes, the poem is highly charged with erotic, even sexual meanings.

The poem unfolds as a series of rhymed verses (**abbcddeeaa**) of either seven or 11 syllables. Arcadelt's polyphony, however, emphasizes the end rhymes only when they align with units of grammatical meaning: as in the strong cadences at "mio" (m. 15), "beato" (m. 24), "desire" (m. 30), and "contento" (m. 43; then prolonged as the canto part sustains the final tone of the melody, while the remaining parts move between sonorities built around B♭ and F). In each of these instances, two of the voice parts move to an octave by way of the closest imperfect consonance (a major sixth). Elsewhere Arcadelt manages to undercut the pattern of rhyme by offering cadences that are equivocal or irregular. In measure 34, the cadential motion occurs between basso and alto, a low registration that has a less than convincing effect in this style, inasmuch as it hides the strong linear motion deep in the musical fabric. (Compare the passage in m. 34 with the cadence in mm. 14–15, for instance.) The first statement of "mio" in measure 10 is similarly equivocal, since in this instance the alto part moves up rather than down (to form the expected unison with the tenore). The repetition of this poetic line is in contrast more emphatic, with a complete cadence between canto and tenore (m. 15).

The most remarkable thing about *Il bianco et dolce cigno*, however, is the way Arcadelt breaks up poetic lines in order to exaggerate and then conflate his two "singing" subjects. In measures 4–5 he brings the upper three voices to a clear cadence at "cantando more"—right in the middle of a poetic line. The gesture allows him to enjamb the remainder of that line of verse with the words of the next verse, "Et io piangendo giung' al fin del viver mio." In case we didn't catch the affective gesture to the extreme "soft" (E♭ and B♭) side of musical space at "piangendo," he repeats the new pairing for added effect (mm. 5–10 and 10–15).

In celebrating the speaker's beatific death with a little too much abandon (at "moro beato"), Arcadelt takes us to another extreme of musical space. We pass through a series of dissonant suspensions to a surprising cadence to D (mm. 21–24); the listener hardly notices the various end-rhymes that fall between "mio" and "beato." But the poet's life (and the piece) cannot end so soon, for having opened this wide musical space between the poet's plaintive "laments" and his imagined "death," Arcadelt quite literally enacts the "thousand" hoped-for deaths in a seemingly endless cascade of imitative entries among the four voices (mm. 34–43). It is a beautiful conclusion to the work, and fits the sense of the text perfectly. Yet this kind of contrapuntal writing was also something of a commonplace in the sixteenth century. Similar passages can be found in many other pieces—for instance, Dentice's Fantasia for solo lute (Anthology 25, esp. mm. 46–50), where a very similar passage stands in precisely the same structural position at the end of the piece.

Arcadelt's madrigal concludes with a special type of "plagal" coda that we have heard before in *Mille regrets* (Anthology 15) and Janequin's *Martin menoit* (Anthology 16). In Arcadelt's piece, an "authentic" contrapuntal cadence is heard between the canto and tenore parts in measures 42–43. But thereafter the canto sustains a long F, while the other parts rock back and forth between sonorities built around B♭ and F, where they at last come to rest in measure 46. The same kind of movement recurs at the end of Dentice's Fantasia, as well as in sacred pieces by Byrd (Anthology 19), Lhéritier (Anthology 20), Palestrina (Anthology 21), Tallis (Anthology 22), and Gesualdo (Anthology 27).

Madonna mia famme bon'offerta

Villanella, 1545

From Adrian Willaert, *Opera Omnia*, ed. H. Zenck et al., Corpus Mensurabilis Musicae, 3 (Rome: American Institute of Musicology, 1950–), 14:160–61.

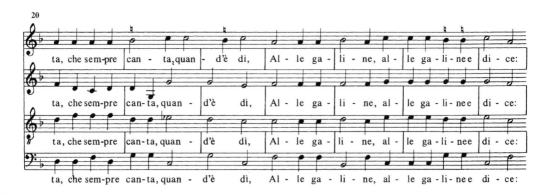

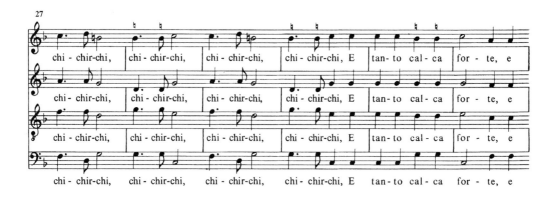

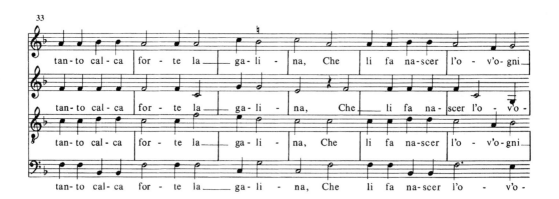

Madonna mia famme bon'offerta,	*My lady, make me a good offer,*
Ch'io porto per presente sto galuccio,	*So I'll give you this fat rooster.*
Che sempre canta quand'è dì	*He's always crowing to tell the hens it's day,*
Alle galline e dice: chi-chir-chi	*"Chi chir chi," he'll always say.*
E tanto calca forte la galina	*And so hard he presses the hen,*
Che li fa nascer l'ov'ogni matina.	*That she lays an egg each morning.*

Quisto mio galo sempre sta al'alerta,	*This bird of mine always stays alert,*
Quando il dì dorme sotto la coperta	*Even in the daytime asleep under cover.*
Che sempre canta quand'è dì	*He's always crowing to tell the hens it's day,*
Alle galline e dice: chi-chir-chi	*"Chi chir chi," he'll always say.*
E tanto calca forte la galina	*And so hard he presses the hen,*
Che li fa nascer l'ov'ogni matina.	*That she lays an egg each morning.*

Presto madonna se lo voi vedere	*Quick, my lady, if you want to see him*
Ca te lo facio mo quisto piacere.	*For I offer you this treat right now.*
Che sempre canta quand'è dì	*He's always crowing to tell the hens it's day,*
Alle galline e dice: chi-chir-chi	*"Chi chir chi," he'll always say.*
E tanto calca forte la galina	*And so hard he presses the hen,*
Che li fa nascer l'ov'ogni matina.	*That she lays an egg each morning.*

The Flemish composer Adrian Willaert was actively mainly in Italy during the middle years of the sixteenth century. Prominent among his output during this time is his *Musica nova* (New Music) of 1559, a collection of motets and madrigals representing the vanguard of the serious style. *Madonna mia famme bon'offerta*, first published in his *Canzone villanesche alla napolitana* of 1545, shows a different side of Willaert's profile as a composer. Such lighthearted songs enjoyed a sudden but lasting vogue in midcentury Italy, both in four-voice vocal versions like the one reproduced here, and in versions for solo voice and lute. The Hilliard Ensemble has recorded Willaert's version for four voices. The ensemble Doulce Memoire has produced a lively arrangement of this piece for voices, lute, and percussion. Other groups have

recorded versions of related villanesche by Diego Pisador (in this case for solo voice and vihuela) and other composers of the Neapolitan orbit.

Given the poem's stanzaic form and the homorhythmic texture of the music, it is under-
standable that Willaert built the harmonies around some basic formulas. The canto and tenore parts generally move in thirds and sixths, except at cadences, where they resolve to a
stable octave, much as in Tromboncino's *Ostinato vo' seguire* (Anthology 13). The alto part generally provides harmonic filler between this pair, and in some respects can be omitted without harming the sense of the whole. Some arrangements of this song for lute (or sometimes
for vihuela) and solo singer leave out the alto in just this way. The basso, in turn, makes alternating thirds and fifths with the tenor. The result sounds and looks to modern musicians
like a series of root-position triads, although Willaert and his contemporaries had no explicit
concept of triadic inversion. The practice recalls sounds heard in the *Ostinato vo' seguire*, and
also in improvisatory traditions of accompaniment or harmonization described by Spanish
musicians like Ortiz (Anthology 24).

The succession of cadences marked out by the canto and tenore mirrors the overall structure of the text. The opening couplet of each stanza shifts rapidly among cadences to F, B♭, and
G. For the refrain (mm. 18–44), Willaert offers a contrasting palette of paired cadences to G
and C; the quoted barnyard cries in measures 27–30 sound to modern ears like dominant and
tonic functions. A final pair of phrases takes us back to the opening orbit around F, this time
with lightly syncopated dissonance in measure 43, as the canto suspends a G over an F in the
basso, then resolves by step.

The first phrase presents special musical problems for editors and performers on account
of the unusual counterpoint and harmony it contains. In this passage the canto and tenore
form a tentative Phrygian cadence to A (mm. 3–4, with the characteristic falling semitone in
the lower of the two voices). Meanwhile, the basso and alto parts make tritone clashes against
the tenor. If this were not enough, just before this the canto part re-sounds A from the previous measure for the first syllable of "mi-a," making a seventh with the tenor. On one hand,
the dissonance could simply be a printer's error. Indeed, one later arrangement of *Madonna
mia famme bon'offerta* for voice and lute makes it clear that the Es in the basso and alto were to
be played as E♭s (thus neutralizing the tritone with the B♭ in the tenor), and that the first of
the B♭s in the tenor should in fact have been a D (thus neutralizing the unprepared seventh
with the canto). On the other hand, the drawn-out dissonance and the exaggerated gesture
it creates hint at another meaning for the opening line of text. Breaking off in the middle of
a word ("Madonna mia fa . . ."), the singers at first seem to say not "My lady make me a good
offer" (as the full line of the poem later has it) but an erotically suggestive double meaning
hidden in the first few syllables: "My lady does." Villanelle are filled with double entendres
like these, which seem perfectly suited to the feigned rustic manner for which the genre was
so prized. Willaert was certainly too careful a composer to have broken the line up in this way
by accident.

Ave verum corpus

Motet, 1605

From William Byrd, *The Byrd Edition*, ed. Philip Brett et al., 17 vols. (London: Stainer & Bell, 1962–2005), 6a:82–86.

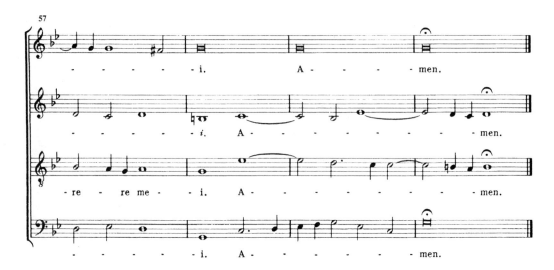

Ave verum corpus,	*Hail, true body*
Natum de Maria Virgine,	*Born of the Virgin Mary,*
Vere passum, immolatum	*That truly suffered, and was sacrificed*
In cruce pro homine;	*Upon the cross for man;*
Cuius latus perforatum,	*From whose pierced side*
Unde fluxit sanguine.	*Flowed blood.*
Esto nobis praegustatum	*Be to us a foretaste*
In mortis examine.	*At death's trial.*
O dulcis, O pie,	*O sweet, O dear,*
O Iesu, Fili Mariae,	*O Jesus, Son of Mary,*
Miserere mei.	*Have mercy on me.*
Amen.	*Amen.*

William Byrd's setting of *Ave verum corpus* first appeared in volume 1 of the *Gradualia* (1605), his great compilation of polyphonic settings of texts for the Propers (that is, the variable parts) of the Catholic liturgy. The text comes from the liturgy for the Feast of Corpus Christi, which was abolished in the English church with the Act of Uniformity in 1559. And so Byrd's fellow Catholics—a beleaguered and often persecuted minority in Anglican England—would have been able to use this motet in religious observances only in private. The Latin text as set by Byrd suggests precisely this, for the last two lines contain a personal supplication, "Have mercy on me," that is not part of the text found in Catholic service books. It is thus perhaps best to understand the setting as a devotional piece that takes its place in a long line of works that give voice to interior spiritual concerns. Like Du Fay's *Ave regina celorum* and Josquin's *Ave Maria . . . Virgo serena*, it speaks for individuals (composers, singers, and listeners alike), even as it weaves a collective polyphonic fabric.

Byrd's motet is punctuated by five musical pauses that coincide with articulations in the liturgical text. The first four of these pauses mark the end-rhymes of each of the four couplets:

"Virgine" (m. 8), "homine" (m. 15), "sanguine" (m. 22), and "examine" (m. 28). The first three cadences are separated from the following phrases by a moment of silence; the fourth cadence (at "Mariae" in m. 35 and again at m. 50) is strong, too, but this one quickly blends into an expansive section for the final supplication and concluding "Amen." Byrd's music thus does a wonderful job of binding the plea for personal forgiveness to the rest of the prayer. The music makes one long, emphatic utterance of what began as an addition to the liturgical text.

Within this broad scheme, all sorts of rich melodic and contrapuntal details call out for our attention. The Phrygian cadence to D between the medius (as the altus part is called in the original source) and bassus at "homine" in measures 14–15, for instance, sets up a highly expressive contrapuntal gesture in the ensuing phrase: the superius makes a dissonant suspension over the tenor as they form another Phrygian cadence, which the bassus nevertheless evades through its own chromatic rise (m. 18). The musical effect is perfectly suited to the text, which recalls Jesus's pierced side.

These plaintive Phrygian gestures are echoed in the final section of the motet, at "Mariae" (in the tenor and bassus parts of mm. 35 and 50). The cascading interplay of descending melodic motives at "miserere mei" (mm. 36–43 and 51–58) seems to amplify the melodic idea heard earlier in the superius at "unde fluxit sanguine" (mm. 19–22). And the crushing cross-relation (in which the F♯ in the superius is followed immediately by an F♮ in the bassus) just as the singers intone "verum" (true, m. 2) recurs later at the exclamatory "O dulcis, o pie, o Iesu" (here presented through the contrast of B♭ with B♮) and at "miserere mei." Considered in the context of the larger social and religious conflict in which Byrd and his fellow secret Catholics were caught, the striking juxtaposition of these different tones seems especially meaningful. The concluding "Amen" offers yet another example of the "plagal" extension found in other compositions (sacred and secular alike) by Josquin (Anthology 15), Janequin (Anthology 16), Arcadelt (Anthology 17), Lhéritier (Anthology 20), Palestrina (Anthology 21), Tallis (Anthology 22), Dentice (Anthology 25), and Gesualdo (Anthology 27). It did not always carry religious connotations. But so frequently was it associated with all kinds of sixteenth-century music that for subsequent periods in music history, the plagal cadence alone was enough to hint at a spiritual topos.

Inasmuch as Byrd has so carefully inscribed these poignant accidental inflections in his printed text, performance of the motet presents none of the problems of *musica ficta* that we have encountered in music written before 1550. Yet much is still left to the discretion of modern performers, especially with respect to pacing and dynamics. The initial choice of performing forces and context for performance can also reveal different aspects of the piece, as one can hear in the many excellent but quite different modern recorded performances. Several in our list of recommended recordings seem especially noteworthy. One by the Tallis Scholars, using a mixed choir of men and women, is richly restrained in its approach to the details we have noted in our analysis. Another, by New York Polyphony, is by comparison quite bold, using a large ensemble of male voices and a very reverberant acoustic that suggests performance in an immense church. A performance by the justly famous Christ Church Cathedral Choir of Oxford (it boasts a 500-year-old choral tradition) uses boy sopranos for the upper line and a male choir for the remaining parts. Their recording puts *Ave verum corpus* in the context of Byrd's other liturgical music for Corpus Christi.

JEAN LHÉRITIER (CA. 1480–AFTER 1551)

Nigra sum
Motet, 1532

From Jean Lhéritier, *Opera Omnia*, ed. Leeman L. Perkins, Corupus Mensurabilis Musicae, 48 (Rome: American Institute of Musicology, 1969), pp. 161–65.

Nigra sum, sed formosa, filia Jherusalem;	*I am black, but beautiful, daughter of Jerusalem;*
ideo dilexit me Dominus,	*and so the Lord has chosen me,*
et introduxit me in cubiculum suum.	*and brought me into his chamber.*

Jean Lhéritier spent much of the 1520s in the service of San Luigi dei Francesi, a church for Rome's French-speaking residents. In the 1530s and early 1540s, Lhéritier worked as chapel master to the cardinal of Clermont at Avignon, in southern France. His career reminds us of the important connections between French and Italian centers of musical patronage during this period, especially among the church elites like cardinals, who maintained households in Rome. Many were ardent supporters of artists, scholars, and musicians. His biography also reminds us that musical life in Rome extended far beyond the famous Papal Chapel. Music was also made in local churches, among communities of foreign residents, and in private aristocratic households.

We do not know when Lhéritier composed *Nigra sum*, but its source tradition no less than Lhéritier's career points toward the international movement of music and musicians that characterized the period. It was first published in the *Motetti del fiore* (Motets of the Flower, 1532), a collection prepared by Jacques Moderne in the French city of Lyons.

Like John Dunstable's *Quam pulchra es* (Anthology 7), the text of *Nigra sum* derives from the biblical Song of Songs. For centuries, excerpts from this erotic dialogue had been incorporated into the Christian liturgy as allegories of divine love (and love for the divine). More specifically, Lhéritier's motet is based on verses from the Song of Songs that were recycled in a plainsong melody sung in honor of the Virgin Mary.

Considered from a musical standpoint, *Nigra sum* is a good example of motet writing of the generation immediately following Josquin des Prez (ca. 1450–1521). To be sure, there are echoes of the varied textures of Josquin's *Ave Maria . . . virgo serena* (Anthology 14): thoroughly imitative counterpoint (as in the opening), short duets (as between tenor II and bassus or superius and altus in mm. 43–48), and brief passages where several voices declaim the text simultaneously (as at "in cubiculum suum," mm. 55–56). In Josquin's *Ave Maria . . . virgo serena* these techniques are presented in rapid succession, and often with an impression of varied rhetorical presentation. In *Nigra sum*, our overall impression is one of continuity, created above all by the great craft with which the composer connects each phrase to the next. There are cadences to mark important words in the prayer (for instance, to D at "formosa" in m. 15, again to D at "Jherusalem" in m. 29, and to G at "Dominus" in m. 41). But in almost every case these articulations are in some way joined immediately to the next set of imitative entries through overlap and anticipation. This smooth, contemplative style became for some composers of the later sixteenth century the very model of sacred counterpoint. Indeed, this particular motet, as we'll see in Anthology 21, was used by Giovanni Pierluigi da Palestrina as the basis of a polyphonic setting of the entire Ordinary of the Catholic Mass. The two works appear together (along with the original plainsong melody of *Nigra sum*) in a modern recording by the Tallis Scholars, making comparison of the motet and its polyphonic elaboration quite easy.

The conclusion of the motet is especially effective. After repeating the words and music for "et introduxit me" (and brought me), Lhéritier suddenly weaves a long series of descending scales and accumulating parallel thirds for the words "in cubiculum suum" (into his chamber, mm. 75–89). Perhaps the gesture was meant as a musical inscription of an allegorical reading that likened the beloved's entry into the king's bedroom as the descent from heaven by the divine presence. (Palestrina used this same music to depict the suffering and burial of Christ in the Credo movement of his *Missa Nigra sum*.) The spiritual wish for the divine now complete, the incessant musical energy dissipates in an extension of the final cadence: the superius and tenor I form a sixth-to-octave cadence in measures 87–88, then sustain a final D while the remaining voices trace movements that fall back to that tone. We encounter this sort of "plagal" cadence frequently over the course of the sixteenth century, in both secular and sacred works by Josquin (Anthology 15), Janequin (Anthology 16), Arcadelt (Anthology 17), Tallis (Anthology 22), Dentice (Anthology 25), Byrd (Anthology 19), and Gesualdo (Anthology 27).

Our edition does not show it, but many ensembles perform the last tone of the superius in measure 87 as C♯ (musica ficta) while simultaneously singing C♮ in the tenor. It is a common contrapuntal situation in five-voice compositions.

Missa nigra sum: Credo

Imitation mass, Before 1590

From Giovanni Pierluigi da Palestrina, *Le opere complete*, ed. Raffaele Casimiri, 31 vols. (Rome: Fratelli Scalera, 1939–65), 15:103–15.

Credo in unum Deum, Patrem
omnipotentem, factorem caeli et terrae,
visibilium omnium et invisibilium.

I believe in one God,
Father almighty, maker of heaven and earth,
and of all things visible and invisible.

Et in unum Dominum Jesum Christum,
Filium Dei unigenitum. Et ex
Patre natum ante omnia saecula.
Deum de Deo, lumen de lumine,
Deum verum de Deo vero.
Genitum, non factum, consubstantialem
Patri: per quem omnia facta sunt.
Qui propter nos homines et propter
nostram salutem descendit de caelis.
Et incarnatus est de Spiritu Sancto ex
Maria Virgine: et homo factus est.
Crucifixus etiam pro nobis: sub
Pontio Pilato passus, et sepultus est.
Et resurrexit tertia die, secundum
Scripturas. Et ascendit in caelum:
sedet ad dexteram Patris.
Et iterum venturus est cum gloria judicare
vivos et mortuos, cujus regni non erit finis.

And in one Lord Jesus Christ, the only-begotten
Son of God Born of the Father before all ages.
God of God, light of light, true God of true God.
Begotten, not made, being of one substance
with the Father, by whom all things were made.
Who for us humans and for our salvation
descended from heaven.
And was made incarnate by the
Holy Spirit of the Virgin Mary,
and was made man.
And was crucified for us;
under Pontius Pilate. He died, and was buried.
And ascended into heaven,
and sits at the right hand of the Father.
And He shall come again
with glory to judge
the living and the dead;
of whose kingdom there shall be no end.

Et in Spiritum Sanctum,
Dominum, et vivificantem: qui ex
Patre Filioque procedit. Qui cum Patre et
Filio simul adoratur et conglorificatur: qui
locutus est per Prophetas.

And in the Holy Spirit, Lord and giver of life,
who proceeds from the Father and the Son.
Who, together with the
Father and the Son, is worshiped and glorified;
who spoke by the prophets.

Et unam sanctam catholicam
et apostolicam Ecclesiam.

And one holy,
Catholic, and Apostolic Church.

Confiteor unum baptisma in
remissionem peccatorum.
Et exspecto resurrectionem mortuorum.
Et vitam ventura saeculi. Amen.

I acknowledge one baptism
for the remission of sins.
And I await the resurrection of the dead.
And the life of the world to come. Amen.

Giovanni Pierluigi da Palestrina was a leading figure in the effort to "purify" Catholic church music in response to the edicts issued after the Council of Trent (1545–63). He composed some 50 "imitation" masses, in which each movement of the Ordinary (Kyrie, Gloria, Credo, Sanctus, and Agnus Dei) reworks the contrapuntal fabric (but not the words) of a polyphonic model. About half of these masses are based on works of other composers. Many of them seem to have been composed fairly early in his career, although some were not published until much later. The *Missa Nigra sum* was first printed in 1590. It takes as its model a five-voice motet by Jean Lhéritier, a French composer who spent much of his career in Rome. (See Anthology 20 for the score of, and commentary on, Lhéritier's *Nigra sum*.) In the discussion below, we will draw close comparisons between Palestrina's and Lhéritier's works. They can be heard together in a performance by the Tallis Scholars, as noted in our list of recommended recordings.

In crafting "imitation" masses, Palestrina and other composers thoroughly reassembled the polyphonic fabric of their models, with new counterpoint, different spacings for imitative entries, and extended points of imitation. In this long Credo movement—a profession of the central tenets of Catholic faith—Palestrina presents the music of Lhéritier's short motet twice, borrowing from strategic points at the beginning, middle, and end in ways that aligned with important parts of the Mass text. The first time through he takes these materials in the order in which Lhéritier presented them: for instance, the music for "Patrem omnipotentem" (following the customary plainsong intonation of "Credo in unum Deum") derives from the first ten measures of *Nigra sum*. Elsewhere, Palestrina refers briefly to the middle of the motet: Lhéritier's measures 31–37 are used for "Et ex Patre" (mm. 27–34), and measures 34–38 of the motet are put to work at "Deum verum" (mm. 40–46).

Nigra sum ends with a striking cascade of descending contrapuntal lines that Palestrina uses to depict the words "descendit de caelis" (came down from heaven). Having reached the end of Lhéritier's motet, Palestrina is now on his own. He pauses for a solemn, chordal presentation of "Et incarnatus est" in measures 74–77. The doctrine of incarnation was of no small importance to Catholics in Palestrina's day. In later generations, officiating priests were asked to bow deeply at this moment in the Mass. The slow motion of Palestrina's polyphony seems to choreograph this reverent gesture in sound.

Now ready to begin again with the process of rehearing the motet, Palestrina returns to the opening measures of *Nigra sum*. The music for the "Crucifixus" section (mm. 92–103; now in four voices rather than the prevailing five) derives from the same opening imitative point that he used for "Patrem omnipotentem" (mm. 1–4). But now the various elements of the motet are taken out of order. The long cascade of descending lines from the end of the model must have seemed ready-made for "passus et sepultus est" (suffered and was buried). Palestrina went immediately to this musical idea without touching on any of the intermediate passages of the motet. (Compare mm. 106–11 of the Credo with mm. 75–79 of *Nigra sum*.) With the idea of "descent" provided by the gesture from Lhéritier's model, Palestrina is ready to supply his own complementary musical representation of the "ascent" of Jesus from the tomb at "et resurrexit," with its high duets and rising lines (mm. 112–17).

The last sections of the Credo call for still different resources, some of them quite independent of the motet. A long passage of homorhythmic writing in triple meter is used for the section beginning at "Et in Spiritum Sanctum, Dominum" (and in the Holy Ghost, Lord), long a favorite for this sort of treatment, given the metrical implications of the text (mm. 166–88). When the text turns toward the unity of the universal church at "Et unam, sanctam, catholicam" (and one holy, Catholic; mm. 189–91), Palestrina seems to lead the charge with a modest duet in which these words are simultaneously presented for all to hear. In closing this section of the Credo, he once again mirrors the closing gestures of *Nigra sum*, with its long descending lines and plagal cadence. We frequently hear this kind of cadential extension in music of the sixteenth century, as noted in our discussions of pieces by Josquin (Anthology 15), Janequin (Anthology 16), Arcadelt (Anthology 17), Byrd (Anthology 19), Tallis (Anthology 22), Dentice (Anthology 25), and Gesualdo (Anthology 27).

The edition of Palestrina's mass reproduced here takes a rather literalist approach to its original sources when it comes to the treatment of accidentals. The frequent B♯s in the score (see the superius in m. 22, for instance) are not really the enharmonic equivalent of C♮s (as they would seem to be for modern readers). In offering what appear to be sharp signs, Palestrina's original typesetter was telling the singers that such Bs were to be solmized as *mi* (B♮ in the modern system). This distinguished these tones from Bs solmized as *fa* (B♭ in the modern system). Modern performers need to be on the lookout for these kinds of conventions, and what they do (and do not) mean. The recording by the Tallis Scholars does just this. It also includes a performance of Lhéritier's *Nigra sum*, and so makes it possible to listen for the connections between the model and the mass in the Credo, and in other movements, too.

22

THOMAS TALLIS (CA. 1505–1585)

Why fumeth in sight

Metrical psalm harmonization, 1567

Edited by Richard Freedman. Modern edition prepared from *The Whole Psalter Translated into English Metre* (London: John Daye, 1567), fols. 22ᵛ–23ʳ. The spelling used in the edition follows the original source. The text transcribed below has been modernized.

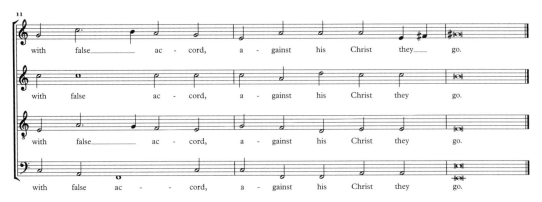

Why fumeth in sight
the Gentiles spite,
in fury raging stout?
Why taketh in hand
the people fond,
vain things to bring about?
The kings arise,
the lords devise,
in counsels met thereto,
Against the Lord
with false accord,
against his Christ they go.

This modest four-voice psalm harmonization comes from a musical appendix that Thomas Tallis crafted for Matthew Parker's *The Whole Psalter Translated into English Metre* (1567). Parker was a central figure in the development of the English Protestant (Anglican) church; as Archbishop of Canterbury from 1559, he disseminated the Thirty-Nine Articles, the basic statement of Anglican faith. Parker's *Whole Psalter* was the first rhyming (thus "metrical") translation of the Book of Psalms, intended for Anglican worship and devotion. It filled a need for music in which every syllable could be distinctly heard and understood. Tallis's model settings offered English Protestants the musical means to participate in sacred song. The metrical basis of the musical setting explains the lack of time signature in the original source and thus in the modern edition. The barring reflects the units of verse, not a fixed musical meter.

Each of Tallis's pieces was meant to exemplify one of the eight "tunes," or church modes. *Why fumeth* represents the third tune, which is to say the first of two centered on E in the traditional paired system of the eight modes described by music theorists (two each on D, E, F, and G). The contours and range of Tallis's tenor part clearly identify the work as belonging to the mode centered on E, with a full octave range above this final tone. Presumably these models were meant to be adapted to other psalms, according to subject matter, although the rhythms would need to be altered to suit each poetic text. In Tallis's setting, the long notes coincide with the rhyming syllables of Parker's translations.

Tallis's tenor part was intended for solo singing in church. The meane (for superius), contratenor (in place of alto), and base (bass) parts were either for use with larger choirs or for performance at home with voices or instruments. Thus Tallis's music hints at a broad range of contexts for pious music-making, both domestic and congregational. This particular harmonization is familiar to modern listeners as the basis of Ralph Vaughan Williams's *Fantasy on a Theme by Thomas Tallis* (1910), composed not long after he completed work as editor of *The English Hymnal* (the standard book of songs for congregational use in Church of England services), in which Tallis's *Why fumeth* can still be found.

In much fifteenth- and sixteenth-century music, the tenor and superius parts of textures like these form a simple duet, moving in parallel sixths and expanding out to a stable octave at cadences. To this pair, composers normally joined a bassus part that moved in alternating thirds and fifths with one or the other of these voices. We encounter this approach most clearly in one of the middle phrases of *Why fumeth*. In measures 7–8 (at the syllables "-rise, the lords devise") the tenor and treble descend in parallel sixths, while the bass traces a series of thirds and fifths with the tenor. The passage sounds strikingly like the romanesca bass familiar from instrumental improvisations of the day (as noted in Chapter 12 of *Music in the Renaissance*).

Elsewhere in Tallis's piece the counterpoint is a little different, on account of both his declamatory approach to the text and the peculiar challenges posed by the mode. On one hand, much of the first six lines of the psalm (mm. 1–6) is given over to a simple declamation of the text, as the tenor part rises up to recite on B. Each phrase comes to a clear stopping place, but none forms a convincing cadence according to the norms of Renaissance counterpoint. In line 7 the tenor at last completes the gradual ascent to E (m. 7, nicely depicting "the kings arise" in the process), then traces a long descent to the original starting tone of E (mm. 8–9).

At this point the harmonization offers a contrapuntal cadence—but not as we might have expected. The tenor and treble parts approach an octave from the closest imperfect consonance (a major sixth; m. 9). In pieces centered on E, however, it is the descending voice that takes the half-step motion (F to E in the tenor), while the treble ascends from D to E by whole step. This is the reverse of what we would find in cadences to D, F, or G, and gives the E, or Phrygian, mode its characteristically tentative sound.

How to craft the counterpoint of the other parts around this motion is yet another challenge. In this context, the bass part cannot accompany the contrapuntal pair just described with a movement of B to E (since the B would form a dissonant tritone with the F in the tenor). Instead it sounds a D, then falls to A for the final sonority of the phrase (m. 11). Meanwhile, the cadential tone E sounds a fifth above this final tone. The effect made perfect sense to Renaissance musicians. To modern listeners it sounds curiously out of place. The final phrase of the piece offers yet another solution to the problem of the Phrygian cadence in polyphonic contexts: the cadential movement in the tenor takes place in measure 12 (F to D to E). Then the other voices sustain a plagal extension through sonorities centered on A and, finally, E.

23

GIOVANNI BASSANO (CA. 1560/61–1617)

Divisions on Orlando di Lasso, *Susanne un jour*

Chansonne spirituelle/diminutions, 1591

Edited by Richard Freedman. Modern edition prepared from Orlando di Lasso, *Mellange d'Orlande de Lassus* (Paris: Adrian Le Roy and Robert Ballard, 1570), fol. 26ᵛ; and from a manuscript copy of Giovanni Bassano, *Motetti, madrigali et canzoni francese* (Venice: Giacomo Vincenti, 1591), p. 33 [missing since World War II], surviving in a manuscript copy prepared by Friedrich Chrysander now in the Staats- und Universitätsbibliothek, Hamburg. The spelling of the literary text given in this modern edition and transcribed below follows the original source.

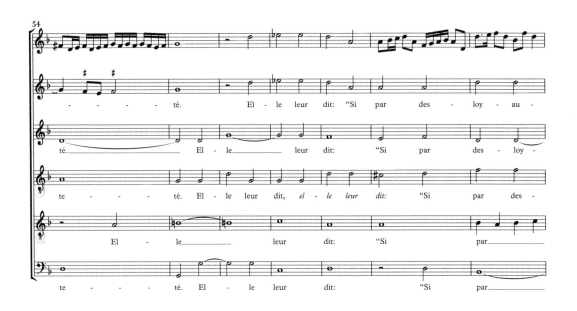

C'est fait de moy, c'est *fait de moy:* si je fay re - sis -
san - ce, C'est fait_____ de moy: si je fay re - sis -
san - ce, C'est fait, c'est fait de moy:_____ si je fay re - sis -
san - ce,_____ C'est fait de moy: si je fay re - sis -
san - ce, C'est fait de moy: si je fay re - sis -

tan - - ce,_____ Vous_____ me fe - rez mou -
tan - - ce, Vous me fe - rez mou - rir_____ en
tan - ce, Vous me fe - rez mou - rir
tan - - ce, Vous me fe - rez mou -
tan - ce, Vous me fe - rez mou - rir_____ en

rir en des - - hon - neur. Mais j'ay - me mieux pé -

des - - - hon - neur. Mais j'ay - me mieux, mas j'ay - me mieux pé -

en des - - hon - neur. Mais j'ay - me mieux, mais j'ay - me

rir en des - hon - neur._____ Mais j'ay - me mieux

des - hon - neur. Mais j'ay - me mieux, mais j'ay - me mieux

rir en in - no - cen - - ce_____ Que

rir en in - no - cen - - ce, pé - rir en in - no - cen - ce Que

mieux, mais j'ay - me mieux pé - rir, pé - rir en in - no - cen - ce Que

pé - rir en in - no - cen - ce_____

pé - rir en in - no - cen - ce_____

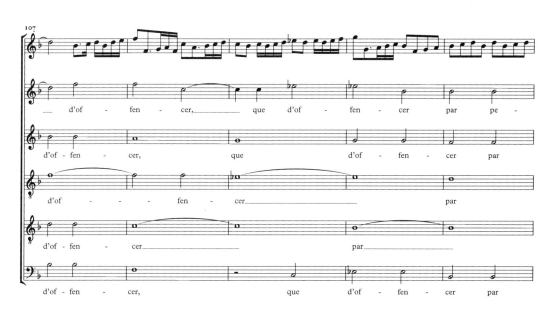

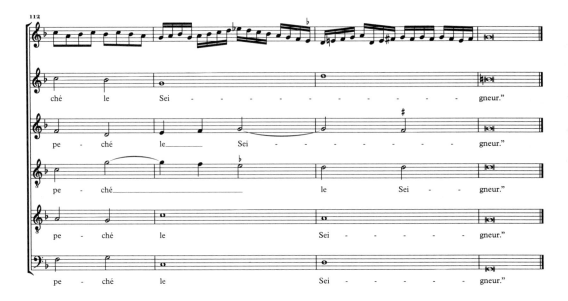

Susane un jour d'amour solicitée	Susanna one day, solicited for love
Par deux vieillards convoitans sa beauté	By two old men lusting for her beauty,
Fut en son coeur triste et déconfortée	In her heart was sad and distressed
Voyant l'effort fait à sa chasteté.	Seeing this attempt upon her chastity.
Elle leur dit: "Si par desloyauté	She said to them: "If by deceit
De ce cors mien vous avez jouissance,	You enjoy this body of mine,
C'est fait de moy; si je fay resistance,	It will be up for me. If I resist,
Vous me ferez mourir en deshonneur.	You will make me die in disgrace.
Mais j'ayme mieux périr en innocence	But I would rather perish in innocence
Que d'offencer par peché le Seigneur."	Than to offend the Lord by sinning."

Giovanni Bassano's virtuosic divisions, or variations, for unspecified solo wind instrument take their place in a long history of arrangements of this sixteenth-century chanson. Appearing in his *Motetti, madrigali, et canzoni francese di diversi eccellentissimi autori* (Motets, Madrigals, and French Canzonas by Various Most Excellent Composers; Venice, 1591), they reveal a musical mind of considerable imagination. Bassano was also a skilled player and served for many years as director of the instrumental ensemble at the Basilica of San Marco in Venice.

Bassano's model was the superius part of Orlando di Lasso's *Susanne un jour*, a spiritual chanson to a text by the Protestant poet Guillaume Guéroult. (In the accompanying score, Bassano's instrumental divisions appear on top of Lasso's song.) It relates the story of the biblical Susanna and her chaste resistance to the sexual assault of the elders. Lasso's work was itself based upon an earlier setting for four voices of the same text by a little-known Protestant composer, Didier Lupi Second, which was printed in Lyons in 1548. It is the most famous of the many hundreds of spiritual chansons (*chansons spirituelles*) sung as domestic entertainment by pious Protestants in French-speaking regions. Lasso's five-voice setting first appeared in an anthology of his music, the *Mellange d'Orlande de Lassus* (Miscellany of Orlando di Lasso), issued by his printer and friend Adrian Le Roy in Paris in 1570. It, too, was well known to musical readers (Catholics and Protestants alike) across late-sixteenth-century Europe. It was frequently reprinted by different publishers, and was often arranged for instruments, as in the case of Bassano's ornamented version considered here.

Lupi's setting, like many chansons from the middle years of the century, is predominantly homorhythmic, with a clear, almost declamatory presentation of the text. It also is quite economical, reusing the same music for each of the first two couplets and again for the last lines of text. Lupi's chanson became famous—his tenor melody was borrowed for a great number of adaptations, rival settings of the same poem, and instrumental versions. Lasso's approach was to weave Lupi's tenor melody into a much richer musical texture of imitative counterpoint for five voices. Lupi's original tenor appears in the superius (starting in m. 1), then again in the quintus, tenor, and bassus parts (mm. 4–12).

Lasso (like Lupi) lavishes special attention on Susanna's statement of defiance at the center of the poem, breaking the seventh line of the text into two parts according to the sense of her words rather than their form. The first half of the line ("I am done for") follows smoothly from the musical material of the previous line. A cadence and a brief moment of silence (mm. 75–76) separate these words from the next ("and if I do resist it"), which belong, both musically and logically, with the following line of verse. In Lasso's setting, the break is further emphasized through a shift to a homorhythmic texture—the only such writing in the entire piece. Perhaps we are meant to hear in it something of Susanna's pious resolve.

Bassano's ornamented version of Lasso's superius adds a further layer of musical complexity to the story of these borrowings. It belongs to a long line of "diminutions," written versions of the decorative improvisations that singers and players were expected to add to vocal lines. (See Ortiz's *Recercada ottava*, Anthology 24, for another example of sixteenth-century diminution practice.) The usual approach to adding these ornaments, to judge from instruction manuals and printed arrangements like this one, was to decorate almost every note with increasingly elaborate runs and patterns. Bassano's version does this with unusual restraint (not every note is decorated) and with a sense of dramatic development. His ornaments have a motivic, almost organic sense about them (listen to the ways in which he repeats and develops diminutions on the opening phrase, for instance), reserving a final burst of energy for the last line of the piece (mm. 107–14). Interestingly, Bassano's interpretation is at its wildest not at the end but at the center of the piece, just where Susanna's defiance is highlighted by Lasso's polyphony: in measure 81, Bassano reverses the direction of Lasso's octave leap, returning to the cadence with a flourish.

In the preface to his collection, Bassano suggests that the remaining parts of Lasso's song be played without ornaments by instruments, or perhaps on a keyboard, with an extra instrument doubling the bassus part. The recorded performance by Musica Antiqua of London gives the ornamented line to a soprano recorder and the remaining voices to lute. This recording also includes Lupi's version of the chanson, as well as ornamented versions of Lasso's piece by Francesco Rognoni Taeggio (second half of sixteenth century—in or after 1626) and Girolamo dalla Casa (?–1601).

24

DIEGO ORTIZ (CA. 1510–CA. 1570)

Recercada ottava
Variations, 1553

Edited by Richard Freedman. The example is from Ortiz's *Trattado de glosas sobre clausulas* (Rome: Dorico, 1553), as printed in an edition otherwise identical in musical contents, but with all of the prefatory and textual commentary in Italian: *Nel qual si tratta delle glose sopra le cadenze* (Rome: Dorico, 1553), fols. 59ᵛ–60ʳ. The cantus, altus, and tenor parts are editorial realizations.

DIEGO ORTIZ

Diego Ortiz was *maestro de capilla* (chapel master) to the Spanish viceroy in Naples during the mid-1500s. Spain sustained a flourishing tradition of music for keyboards and fretted string instruments (some played with bows, others without) during the fifteenth and sixteenth centuries. Keyboardists in Italy, Germany, and England all knew of the important music of Ortiz, Antonio de Cabezón, and other Spanish players. The lute and its bowed counterpart, the viol, each borrowed heavily from the repertory and design of the Spanish vihuela de mano.

Ortiz's two-volume treatise on ornamentation, the *Trattado de glosas sobre clausulas* (Treatise of Elaborated Cadences), was issued in both Spanish and Italian editions in Rome in 1553. In the first volume, he offers practical advice for the improvising string player, illustrated by formulaic models for decorating cadences and elaborating melodic intervals with busy diminutions like those in Giovanni Bassano's version of *Susanne un jour* (see Anthology 23). *Glosas*, however, were a genre in their own right, consisting of variations on a given theme, and can be found throughout the Spanish keyboard tradition. The *recercada* was another kind of piece favored by Spanish instrumentalists. In it, a composer might take a motet, madrigal, or chanson as a point of departure, or even create his own contrapuntal framework for improvisation. The second volume of Ortiz's treatise offers these sorts of pieces, including decorated arrangements of a famous madrigal (Jacques Arcadelt's *O felici occhi miei* [O My Happy Eyes]) and a famous chanson (Pierre Sandrin's *Doulce memoire* [Sweet Memory]) for various solo viols with ensemble or keyboard accompaniment. There are also sets of variations (elsewhere called *differencias*, but here somewhat confusingly labeled *recercadas*) on various standard melodies (*tenores*). The *Recercada ottava* (Eighth Recercada) is drawn from this set.

Like the other Italian tenor patterns found in Ortiz's book, the *Recercada ottava* unfolds in a series of balanced, parallel phrases, in groups of eight or four measures (the double bars are original to the bass part). The overall form might be diagrammed as two statements of the pattern **AABBCC**, with the **A** section consisting of eight measures and the **B** and **C** sections of four. In addition to the global repetition of this 32-measure design, there is a great deal of repetition within and among the individual phrases, which rely on basic but highly varied contrapuntal formulas.

The tenor and cantus melodies of Ortiz's other accompaniments from the *Trattado* normally move in parallel sixths within a narrow, conjunct range. The bassus part makes a series of alternating harmonic thirds and fifths with the tenor (as seen in Ex. 12.2 in *Music in the Renaissance*, an excerpt from another of Ortiz's recercadas, for which he wrote out all three of the accompanying lines). In the case of the *Recercada ottava*, Ortiz provides only the bassus part plus its ornamented elaboration; we have used the norms set forth in his other pieces to realize the harmonies indicated in small noteheads in our modern edition for the tenor, altus, and cantus voice parts. The results sound to modern listeners like a series of root-position triads, albeit ones that seem to wobble in their orientation between G and B♭ as a "tonic." The ends of the phrases nevertheless come to rest convincingly on D and G. Ortiz and his contemporaries did not consider the concept of triadic inversion, nor did they explain musical motion through the calculus of functional harmony. Yet this piece, like some of Ortiz's other arrangements of Italian tenors, sounds surprisingly modern and can be described using the symbol system of roman-numeral harmony.

Ortiz's sample ornaments for the solo viola da gamba join a long tradition of instrumental and vocal diminution practice in the sixteenth century. His aim seems to be to show the aspiring player how to join various melodic formulas with the underlying tenor and bassus pair. In measures 3–5, for instance, the solo viol begins on the same tone as the bassus, in each case applying the same turning figure to animate the line. Similar repetitions and echoes of relatively simple ideas can be heard in the compressed fanfare at measures 40–42 and the echo effects in measures 43–46. These diminutions, as the term suggests, are better understood as rhythmic rather than melodic ornaments. Because the viols and harpsichord were very limited in their dynamic range, these repeated articulations may also have served a dynamic and accentual purpose.

Given the didactic character of Ortiz's treatise, we should probably feel free to take his models as points of departure rather than finished works. Different modern performers offer individual perspectives on the score. The performance by the ensemble Charivari Agréable takes a collective approach to diminution. In this case, a solo viola da gamba is joined by lute and chamber organ. Jordi Savall, a viola da gamba virtuoso who has thoroughly explored the literature for improvising composers of the sixteenth through the eighteenth centuries, uses varied movements of the bow to give shape and energy to the different melodic motives. He is accompanied by lute and harpsichord, each of which improvises simultaneously with him.

25

FABRIZIO DENTICE (?1539–1581)

Fantasia

Fantasia, 1560s

From *Neapolitan Lute Music: Fabrizio Dentice, Giulio Severino,Giovanni Antonio Severino, Francesco Cardone*, ed. John Griffiths and Dinko Fabris, Recent Researches in the Music of the Renaissance, 140 (Middleton, WI: A-R Editions, 2004), pp. 94–95.

Fabrizio Dentice was a singer, lutenist, and composer active in Naples, Rome, and Parma during the middle years of the sixteenth century. He was also a member of a Neapolitan noble family. In light of the bias against professional musicians reflected in works like Baldassare Castiglione's *Book of the Courtier*, it is not surprising that his music was never printed during his lifetime. Instead, it circulated in manuscripts prepared for private performances by the gentlemen and courtiers with whom Dentice associated.

The main source for Dentice's music is a book of tablature known as the Siena Lute Book, now preserved in the Netherlands Music Institute in The Hague. It contains, in addition to Dentice's solo fantasias, a cross-section of music made for and adapted to the solo lute. There are fantasias and ricercars by men like Francesco da Milano; variations on the famous basse danse tenor *La Spagna*, and intabulations for lute of chansons by various northern and French composers, including Orlando di Lasso's *Susanne un jour* (see Anthology 23).

Dentice was by all accounts a very accomplished performer, composer, and improviser. This fantasia bears out that testimony. It touches on commonplaces of musical language of the mid-sixteenth century: leisurely points of imitation, densely woven motivic counterpoint, and a variety of formulaic cadences. There are also references to dance music and flashes of virtuosic diminutions (decorative scales and turns) that singers and instrumentalists loved to apply to the music they performed.

Dentice's piece rewards careful analysis, both for its variety and for its subtle coherence. It opens with a broad point of imitation at the lower fifth, suggesting four independent voices in which the same lyrical, triadic melody is passed in turn from superius to altus, from altus to tenor, and from tenor to bassus. This imitative texture is common in vocal music of the period, secular and sacred alike; see, for instance, Jean Lhéritier's motet *Nigra sum* (Anthology 20).

Arriving at a solid cadence to C in measure 10 (a fifth away from the F-based opening motive), Dentice is ready to begin again with an elaborated repetition of the same contrapuntal fabric. Here the order of entries is different (bassus, superius, then bassus again). So, too, the tonal space expands, as when the main idea starts on G (in the bassus register in m. 13), instead of being confined to F or B♭. This in turn sets up what sounds like a cadence to G in measure 15, although the gesture is thwarted by the bassus, which moves up to E♭ as the superius and tenor expand out to G. (The mid-sixteenth-century theorist Gioseffo Zarlino would have called this an "evaded" cadence; modern terminology prefers "deceptive.")

Dentice now takes up the opening idea again, this time presenting it in the tenor (m. 16) on the original position on F. But soon he abandons the main tune in favor of a series of densely packed entries of a turning motive (beginning in the superius at m. 18) that ricochet through the contrapuntal fabric, each one a fourth below the last. The effect is something like an episode in an eighteenth-century fugue. This passage moves toward a formulaic cadential flourish around F (m. 23). Once again Dentice thwarts closure at the last instant, as the bassus moves to D, just as the superius and tenor expand out to their expected F. A fourth section (mm. 23–30) refers once again to the main theme, although it is now highly elaborated with decorative diminutions that fill in the gaps and break up the held notes of the tune.

Up to this point, all of the devices Dentice uses have been consistent with the instrumental fantasia as developed by Francesco da Milano (1497–1543) and others starting in the 1530s. But the sudden shift to triple meter and the hints of homorhythmic dance music at measure 30 point instead toward the instrumental *canzona alla francese*, a kind of ensemble piece (normally for viols) modeled on the French chanson, with its patchwork of contrasting textures and meters.

Dentice, however, seems not to have been content with the periodic regularity typical of triple-meter interludes. Beginning at measure 37, this homorhythmic section transforms itself into a contrapuntal dance. The cascade of turning figures in dotted rhythms, like the closely spaced entries of a fugal stretto, prepares the ground for the climactic coda (mm. 43–51), in which Dentice piles up a similarly dense series of entries with a motive that leaps up a fourth, then gently falls by steps. In this, and in the relaxing plagal close to F by way of B♭, Dentice's fantasia recalls a similar passage at the end of Jacques Arcadelt's madrigal *Il bianco e dolce cigno* (see Anthology 17). Saving the soprano entry for the last (mm. 49–50), Dentice's lute appears to go out singing, like Arcadelt's dying swan and poet. The piece also ends with a plagal cadence of the sort we hear in other pieces of the sixteenth century, including works by Josquin (Anthology 15), Janequin (Anthology 16), Arcadelt (Anthology 17), Byrd (Anthology 19), Lhéritier (Anthology 20), Palestrina (Anthology 21), Tallis (Anthology 22), and Gesualdo (Anthology 27).

The Siena Lute Book is in tablature, so while it shows the performer exactly where to place the fingers on the fretboard, and which strings to pluck when, it tells the player almost nothing about the polyphonic fabric that rests behind the diagrams. The lutenist must infer these voice parts and play them in such a way that the listener will have the impression of contrapuntal interplay. Given the intimate, perishable sound of the lute, this must be done in large measure by the careful application of rhythmic nuance. Diminutions are another way to lend emphasis to particular passages (especially cadences), for in striking and restriking the strings, the player produces a dynamic accent and welling up of sound that are not otherwise possible with a single note. The masterful performance by Jacob Heringman (drawn from a CD that offers selections taken entirely from the Siena Lute Book) meets the challenge nicely.

26

CLAUDIO MONTEVERDI (1567–1643)

Sfogava con le stelle
Madrigal, Published 1603

From Claudio Monteverdi, *Il quarto libro di madrigali a cinque voci*, ed. Gian Francesco Malipiero, Tutte le opere di Claudio Monteverdi, 17 vols. (Bologna: Enrico Venturi, 1926–68), 4:15–19.

Sfogava con le stelle
un inferno d'amore
sotto notturno ciel il suo dolore,
e dicea fisso in loro:
"O imagini belle
de l'idol mio ch'adoro,
sì com'a me mostrate
mentre così splendete
la sua rara beltate,
così mostrast'a lei
i vivi ardori miei.
La fareste col vostr'aureo sembiante
pietosa sì come me fate amante."

Unburdening himself to the stars
In an inferno of love,
Beneath a night sky, he vented his sorrow,
And gazing upon them, said:
"O lovely images
Of the goddess I adore,
Since you show me
With such splendor
Her rare beauty,
If only you could reveal to her
The intensity of my passion
You could make her, with your golden countenance,
As compassionate as you have made me amorous."

Claudio Monteverdi's *Sfogava con le stelle*, from his *Fourth Book of Madrigals for Five Voices* of 1603, connects old practices in both sacred and secular music with new aesthetic priorities of the seventeenth century. Its poetic text describes and then quotes the poignant cries of a lover who appeals to the stars to assuage a broken heart. Monteverdi deploys the old tradition of liturgical recitative, falsobordone, an Italian version of the improvised harmonization of plainchant we have heard in pieces like *There is no rose* (Anthology 8) and Guillaume Du Fay's *Supremum est mortalibus* (Anthology 9). Practices like falsobordone, faburden, and fauxbourdon were not only practical techniques for the observance of the divine liturgy; they could also be used to invoke the sacred, even in secular contexts like the madrigal. At the same time, the recitational rhythms, in which the singers are instructed to freely declaim the texts over chordal harmonies, point to the new form of operatic recitative known as the *stile rappresentativo* (theatrical style), of which Monteverdi himself was an important and early practitioner, as Wendy Heller explains in *Music in the Baroque*. *Sfogava con le stelle* also calls upon conventions of the serious and not-so-serious madrigal of the sixteenth century, deploying imitative counterpoint for five voices, short sections for reduced textures of three singers, and melodic ornaments of a sort that we have encountered many times in works by composers of the sixteenth century, from Jacques Arcadelt's *Il bianco e dolce cigno* (Anthology 17) to Adrian Willaert's *Madonna mia famme bon'offerta* (Anthology 18) and Luca Marenzio's *Liquide perle* (Anthology 1).

The poem—attributed by some to Ottavio Rinuccini, an early opera librettist—consists of various combinations of seven- and 11-syllable lines, combined in a loose rhyme scheme. At the largest level, Monteverdi juxtaposes the narrator's four-line introduction (in falso-bordone recitative) with the lyrical outpourings of the speaker (in a variety of contrapuntal idioms). He returns to the falsobordone texture in the closing lines of the text, just as the speaker's prayer becomes most earnest. The reprise lends a certain symmetry to the piece, cadencing to a final sonority on D, where it began.

The textural reprise also highlights the crucial connection between the speaker's pain ("dolore," mm. 8–10) and the urgency with which he seeks his beloved's compassion ("pietosa," repeatedly, and with increasing emphasis, in m. 46 to the end). In each of these highly expressive passages, Monteverdi pushes the traditional contrapuntal language to its limits, with many dissonances among the parts. In measure 8, for instance, the canto makes an unprepared second with the quinto below it. And while the first statement of "pietosa" in measure 46 seems relatively tame (if rhythmically emphatic), by measure 64 it is positively wild, with unprepared dissonance between the canto and tenore and among the quinto, te-nore, and basso parts. In short, Monteverdi uses expressive dissonance to bind together the two parts of the poem, one narrative, the other lyrical.

In other ways, too, Monteverdi carefully stages poetic images and syntax throughout the piece. Lines of poetry are both joined together and set off from one another by means of contrasting textures and punctuating cadences. Two cadences to D signal the end of the second and third verses (mm. 5 and 10). The end of the narrator's introduction is also marked by a cadence, now moving out to establish new tonal space by pausing expectantly on C (m. 14). This sonority in turn leads seamlessly into the first lyrical outpouring of ornamented lines in contrapuntal motion.

Moving from one tradition of improvisation (falsobordone) to another (diminution), Monteverdi's sweeping lines in contrary motion seem to paint an entire skyscape before our ears. From this point forward, the short seven-syllable lines are repeated by contrasting choirs of small groups of voices (sometimes three, sometimes four) in textures drawn from the world of light genres like the canzonetta (as represented by Marenzio's *Liquide perle*). All of this culminates in the cadence to F in measure 44. From here it is but a slight turn to the closing prayer and the reprise of the falsobordone texture heard at the outset of the piece.

The score reproduced in our anthology comes from an edition prepared during the early years of the twentieth century by the Italian composer and musicologist Gian

Francesco Malipiero. It includes dynamic markings that were never part of the original prints. Of course, modern performers will need to make their own judgments about how to shape their interpretations. The recording by Delitiae Musicae uses instrumental accompaniment throughout, introducing the madrigal with a wildly imaginative prelude. Nothing in Monteverdi's original collection of madrigals suggests either the prelude or the accompaniment, although in fact we know that singers were sometimes joined by a lutenist or keyboard player who played along with the vocal parts or even ornamented them while others sang. Indeed, starting with the second half of Monteverdi's *Fifth Book of Madrigals* (published in 1605), instrumental accompaniments became an explicit part of a new compositional approach known as the "continuo madrigal." Such pieces were in turn allied with a new emphasis on solo song during the early decades of the seventeenth century. There was ample precedent during the sixteenth century for the tradition of arranging polyphonic works for one or two singers plus instrumental accompaniment. But composers of the early seventeenth century embraced this ideal as the perfect vehicle for the delivery of the many images and moods of their chosen literary texts, as Wendy Heller observes in *Music in the Baroque.*

27

CARLO GESUALDO (CA. 1561–1613)

O vos omnes, from Tenebrae for Holy Week

Motet, 1611

From Carlo Gesualdo, *Sämtliche Werke*, ed. Glenn Watkins and Wilhelm Weismann, 10 vols. (Hamburg: Ugrino, 1957), 7:80–82.

RESPOND

O vos omnes qui transitis per viam,   *All you who pass by along the way,*
attendite, et videte: *behold, and see*
si est dolor similis sicut dolor meus.   *if there is any sorrow like my sorrow.*

VERSE

Attendite universi populi et videte   *Behold, all people and see my sorrow.*
dolorem meum.

Carlo Gesualdo is famous for his extremely chromatic and expressive madrigals. This composition, from his *Tenebrae for Holy Week* (1611), represents a lesser-known side of his output, although it shares the musical aesthetic of those secular compositions. Demanding much from the singers, and no less from listeners, this intensely moving motet was among the first pieces issued in score, with all parts in vertical alignment, rather than in the partbook format normally used in publications of vocal polyphony.

The *Tenebrae* are responsorial hymns sung as part of the Catholic liturgy observed on Thursday, Friday, and Saturday evenings immediately before Easter. As the term suggests, these "responsories" were traditionally sung in plainsong by two contrasting groups of singers: the full choir for the refrain (or respond) and a soloist or small group for the verses. Eventually the refrains were shortened, and quite often the number of verses reduced to one. The *Tenebrae* responsories all follow this abbreviated scheme: the respond itself, a verse, then a repetition of the second half of the respond. The overall form might thus be diagrammed **ABCB**, where **B** is the second half of the response.

Gesualdo's polyphonic motets do not quote the plainsong melody for the *Tenebrae* cycle. But they do follow the responsory form exactly. Thus after the verse the singers return to measure 15 of the response, then stop at the conclusion of that section (m. 31). Indeed, modern ensembles like the Tallis Scholars featured in our list of recommended recordings recall the old responsorial form, using soloists for the verse (mm. 32–42 in the case of this motet) and a full choir for the rest of piece. Yet even as it follows the basic form of its liturgical text, Gesualdo's setting sounds anything but conventional, as the respond and verse are broken up, repeated, and amplified almost beyond verbal comprehension.

O vos omnes is especially striking for its chromaticism, both within individual voice parts and across the ensemble. As in many of the composer's secular madrigals, these chromatic lines involve cross-relations (as in the first two measures of this piece, where a D♮ in the superius part is followed by a D♯ in the sexta pars), as well as direct chromaticism in a single voice (as when the quintus moves from G to G♯ in m. 5). Presented in close harmony and declamatory rhythms, the effects can be both deeply moving and deeply unsettling.

Having managed in the **A** section (up to m. 15) to command the attention of those who might be tempted merely to "pass by" (in the words of the liturgical text), Gesualdo turns in the remainder of the motet to the representation of Jesus's sufferings. In contrast to the largely declamatory textures of the first part of the piece, the relationship among the six voices is often densely contrapuntal. The resulting harmonies are almost literally excruciating, although there are relatively few unprepared dissonances of the sort found in Claudio Monteverdi's *Sfogava con le stelle* (see Anthology 26).

For all Gesualdo's mannered novelty, *O vos omnes* includes some surprisingly conventional figures: The descending Phrygian tetrachord in the superius part at "dolorem meum" (mm. 40–42) is familiar from any number of sixteenth-century laments, such as John Wilbye's *Draw on, sweet Night* (Anthology 12) or *Mille regrets* (Anthology 15). A version of this same figure is also heard in the **B** section (at "dolor similis" in the superius part of mm. 21–23). The gently sliding parallel harmonies and dissonant suspensions among the three upper voices can be heard as a chromatic version of the old fauxbourdon tradition. And at the very end of the **B** section (it is also the last thing we hear in this motet), there is a plagal cadence (at "meus" in mm. 29–30), although the weird series of what sound like major and minor triads in the approach to the cadence make it more strange than familiar.

An unsettling mix of the conventional and the experimental, *O vos omnes* highlights the competing tensions at work in Gesualdo's musical idiom, even as it perfectly fulfills its liturgical function. It reminds us of the many ways in which the newest sounds of secular chamber music could be enlisted in the expression of intense religious sensibilities.

NOTES ON VOICE ROLES AND NAMES USED IN THE MODERN EDITIONS

Early fifteenth-century sources sometimes designate voice parts according to the old hierarchical model of functions established in the thirteenth and fourteenth centuries: *tenor* for the slow-moving cantus firmus, then *motetus* and *triplum* for the upper voices that carry the text.

Nevertheless, most fifteenth-century sources use *cantus* for any of the upper voices, especially ones carrying the text of a composition. The tenor forms an essential counterpoint with the cantus.

Depending on the texture, we also find various *contratenor* (or simply *contra*) voices. To distinguish them by range, they were sometimes called *contratenor bassus, contratenor altus*, and *contratenor superius*. These in turn where shortened to *bassus, altus,* and *superius.*

Sixteenth-century sources retain these basic terms, either in Latin or in related Italian terms: *basso, alto, tenore, soprano*. Compositions in five or six parts simply named the additional voices accordingly: *quintus* (or *quinto, quinta*) and *sextus* (or *sexta*).

English sources sometimes use special terms to designate the conventional voice roles: *burden* or *meane* in place of superius, or *medius* in place of altus. *Bass* is used for bassus.

Fauxbourdon (sometimes *faulxbourdon* or *faburden*) is used by modern editors to designate unwritten voice parts that were sometimes added in performance, as explained in the commentaries.